OR YOUR MONEY BACK

OR YOUR MONEY BACK

For the Business Executive, Student,
or Man on the Street...
a Practical Way to Turn
a Minimum Investment into a Fortune
Using Broadcast Advertising

by ALVIN EICOFF

Crown Publishers, Inc.
New York

Manufactured in the United States of America

Library of Congress Cataloging in Publication Data
Eicoff, Alvin.
Or your money back.
1. Television advertising.   2. Radio advertising.
I Title.
HF6146.T42E35 1982   659.14   82-5020
ISBN: 0-517-547392   AACR2

10 9 8 7 6 5 4 3 2 1
First Edition

Contents

Contents

Photographs appear following page 74

Introduction

Some people in America hate advertising.

They dislike the inane jingles, the feeble attempts at humor, and the tastelessness of many commercials. They rue the advertising that interrupts their favorite programs or that takes up precious space in their magazines. With unbridled passion, they despise Mr. Whipple, detest the Man from Glad, and would love to see Mrs. Olsen get a pie in the face.

Nor is that kind of advertising my cup of tea! That might seem a strange thing, for I have spent my entire life in this business. But my approach to advertising bears little resemblance to the mainstream approach. In fact, others in the industry view me as a heretic.

Because of that, I expect this book to be criticized in New York agencies, ostracized in Chicago's, and vilified in L.A. shops. God forbid if one of their clients should see it! They might find out that their multimillion-dollar advertising budget isn't worth the paper it's printed on.

For years, a certain segment of the advertising industry has been guilty of spinning ads out of whole cloth; they place a premium on advertising's appearance, not on the

1

reality of sales. The result: too many ads and commercials that resemble third-rate vaudeville, desperately trying to attract an audience with stale jokes and chorus lines.

I'm writing this book with the hope that advertising can be taken out of the hands of the entertainers and returned to its proper place. That place is firmly rooted in American salesmanship: the good, hard sell is as much a part of this country as apple pie. The salesman has always had a special place in our history: the carnival barker, the Fuller Brush man, the guy on the road with nothing but a suitcase and a smile. To translate the romance, the style of those time-honored salesmen to advertising is what my career has been dedicated to.

I realize that there have been many books written about advertising. How many ad agency presidents have penned epic tomes about their salad days in the wild and woolly world of buy-and-sell? I guarantee you that this book will be nothing like those self-congratulatory memoirs. I am not going to waste your time reciting all the clever ads I've written or write chapters on ''how to be creative.''

No, this book won't treat advertising like an elegant, beautiful lady, touching only on that radiant, glowing exterior. Rather, it will get to its hot-blooded, scheming soul.

I'll tell you how to turn a million-dollar idea into a million dollars; explain why advertising works best during certain times of the day and days of the week; detail where the money is to be made on cable TV.

My goal, quite simply, is to help people finally understand the power and the glory of advertising.

I intend to tell advertising's story through my own eyes. I suppose I could do this book journalistically, interviewing people in the business and writing a thoughtful, objective analysis of the advertising world. But that's not my style. I am not objective about anything.

I'm going to challenge many of the self-important advertising executives who give salesmanship a bad name. If the chapters in this book make their blood boil, I'll know the effort has been worth it. I'm not doing this because I want to become the Ralph Nader of the advertising industry. No, I write this because I love and respect my profession. On its most basic level, that profession involves taking a product, studying it, learning what's unique about it, and then presenting that "uniqueness" so that the consumer is motivated to buy the product.

But on another level, advertising is more than that. It is one of the few things left that allows the small businessman to dream: to dream of taking his invention to market and striking it rich. There are literally thousands of inventors in this country (many of them visit our offices each week) with innovative, beneficial products and ideas and no way to market them. Oh, perhaps a major company will offer to buy their invention for a paltry sum, but that is not part of their dream. Nor is their dream the humiliation they suffer when they go to a big advertising agency with their product, only to be laughed out of the office. Advertising has become so costly and complex, they don't have a chance.

At A. Eicoff & Company, we give them that chance. Though we are one of Chicago's larger agencies with major, corporate accounts, we still believe advertising is a viable outlet for the small businessman—especially television advertising. How we have turned dreams into multimillion-dollar success stories is part of what this book is about.

But this book is for other people as well. It's for the Fortune 500 executive who is looking at his budget and wondering why he spent $15 million for a new product introduction that failed miserably. And it's for the industrial manufacturer who wants to market his industrial product to the consumer but can't figure out how to do it.

Finally, and perhaps most important, it's for the guy on the street who doesn't know beans about advertising. If you talk to him about positioning, he'll think you are talking about sex. But advertising is a part of his life—he can't turn on the TV or walk down the street without it hitting him in the face. I'd like to give that guy a behind-the-scenes look at what it's all about. I'd like to tell him a tale or two about the early days of television advertising when a "pitchman" would have thirty minutes to hawk his goods. And I'd like to introduce him to some of the outrageous characters who'd sell their mother if they thought they could make a profit.

Perhaps then that guy will have a better understanding of what advertising was, is, and will be. Perhaps then he will understand who's trying to sell him a bill of goods and who's trying to sell good products for a few bills.

For years, friends and business associates have been urging me to write a book. They have insisted that I have a story to tell that has never been told before—not only the story of my maverick career, but the story of the myths and realities of advertising in the past forty years. They have emphasized that this story will prove educational to anyone who has anything to do with advertising: from students interested in advertising as a career to seasoned professionals searching for a fresh perspective on the business.

So, I have written this book, even though I am primarily a writer of copy, not books. I have written it the way I believe advertising should be written—straightforward, logically, and packed full of information that will be of use to the consumer. I have detailed what I did, why I did it, what the results were, letting the chips fall where they may. If the book has any one purpose, it is to stimulate readers to reassess the traditional beliefs about advertising, to think about what factors produce good advertising.

Good advertising is difficult to define. I've always thought that at its best it achieves the perfection of a Japanese haiku. Like that poetic form, it conveys information simply and directly in a limited space and time. The late Leo Burnett was a practitioner of this method of advertising. He was not a Fancy Dan. His philosophy can be summed up by his observations on what some would call a "primitive" ad.

"One time I saw a sign in a yard near a lake, which read WORMS WITH FISH APPEAL. I think that was an excellent ad for its purpose."

To the amateur advertiser who created that sign, I dedicate this book.

1

Take That, You Dirty Rat

As a young man, I arrived in Chicago in the forties with a little advertising experience but uncertain as to where that experience would take me. But once I met Lee Ratner, I found myself in the world of direct-response advertising.

At first, I didn't know what to make of this fast-talking diamond in the rough who told me he had sold glow-in-the-dark gardenias through mail-order radio during World War II. He added that he would give me a call soon, explaining that he might have a product that was right for me.

A few weeks later he called. He told me about a fly spray that, with one application, would kill all the flies in a house for an entire year. Though the product intrigued me, its price did not. Ratner wanted to sell it for $2.98, whereas most fly sprays went for about 69 cents. I tried every way I knew to get him to buzz off. But he continued plaguing me with phone calls, and finally I agreed to write radio copy for his product, which we dubbed Flypel. I wrote the copy, showed it to Ratner, and he said, "Terrific, buy me some time." I said, "Sure," and prayed that Flypel and Ratner would go away. They didn't. I wanted to spray my phone with anti-Ratner lotion, ridding me of that ringing sensation I heard when he called five times daily. Ultimately, I decided that the only way to get rid of him was to buy some time and let the product flop. I had heard that the "Suppertime Frolics," a program on Chicago's WJJD, had some time open that summer. The time they offered me, however, was expensive: thirteen weeks at $300 a week. When I told Ratner we would have to buy all thirteen weeks (which was a white lie meant to discourage him), I assumed he'd say forget it, not having that kind of money available. I was therefore surprised when he showed up at my office the next day and laid four $1,000 bills on my desk and said, "Buy it." I was impressed. I probably would have been less impressed if I had known that Ratner had hocked his car to get that money.

Flypel's success was fast and furious. We started buying time on stations across the country and in Mexico, and the demand for the product was enormous. On one station alone, we were getting an incredible seven thousand orders a week. Ratner was making over $15,000 a week net profit on the one station and he was on over two hundred fifty stations. Orders were dropping like flies on Ratner's desk.

The commercial I wrote for Flypel was written in a matter of minutes. I sat down at the typewriter and pounded on the keys like Gene Krupa on drums. The words carried a rhythm all their own. Perhaps what I wrote was unsophisticated by modern advertising standards. But sophistication sells diamonds and minks, not fly spray. I was a neophyte copywriter, and my Flypel copy was far from perfect. But it had something that most radio commercials of the time didn't have: it hit the consumer right where he lived. The commercial didn't plead for customers to buy the product and it didn't try to be cute. It challenged the listener not to buy the product. It was so bold and brassy that you couldn't help but order Flypel. It worked so well because I managed to scare the hell out of the listeners; I made flies into a deadly enemy that only Flypel could destroy. Here's a portion of what I wrote:

Friends, now you can do away with America's number one public enemy—the common housefly and mosquito! Scientists have known for years that flies carry dangerous diseases such as typhoid fever and dysentery. Now, scientists believe that the common fly transmits the dreaded polio virus. The polio season is here—and the U.S. Bureau of Health, in its precautionary bulletin on polio, recommends the elimination of the housefly as well as the mosquito and other insects as a safety measure! Flypel, a great new chemical discovery, now makes it possible for you to rid your home of flies and mosquitos with one application. Yes, one application of Flypel will keep your home relatively fly-free for weeks! . . . IT'S THE GREATEST INSECTICIDE DISCOVERY EVER! Now, for the first time, we are offering this product to the general public at a price competitive to any insecticide on the market. We guarantee that one application of Flypel will keep your home free of flies, or your money back!

The commercial used hyperbole like a sword, and $2.98 seemed a small price to pay to kill the haunting, horrible specter of the deadly housefly.

When the summer ended, so did the demand for Flypel. But Ratner, still intent on mass murder, turned his killer instinct toward rodents. He had heard that the University of Wisconsin was doing research on an anticoagulant called warfarin. Their research also showed that warfarin was terrific for killing rats. In addition, rats failed to develop an immunity to warfarin as they had to a number of other products. And research showed that humans or other animals wouldn't die from it unless they ingested huge quantities of the stuff. Ratner obtained rights to the product, and told me he wanted to sell it for $2.98, the same price as Flypel. To this day, I'm convinced he chose that number because it was the same as the Flypel price. And again, there were many other rat poisons on the market that sold for considerably less. When I pointed this out to him, he responded with Ratner's Rule: Price a product according to what it does, not what it looks like or costs to make. He explained that "If you don't got rats, two dollars ninety-eight cents might seem like a lot. But if you got a bunch of those furry fellows crawling around your home, you'll pay anything to get rid of 'em."

The next step was to give our rat killer a name. Naming a product correctly is crucial to a product's success. If you want people to have certain expectations about a product, the name should fulfill those expectations. It is like naming a child. If you have a boy and you hope he will be a star athlete, you don't name him Clarence or Arthur. Butch, Spike, or Danny are tougher, harder-sounding names. So we racked our brains trying to come up with an appropriate name for the rat killer. At first, we played around with X names: Rat-X, Rid-X, and the like, the X conveying a sinister, ominous power. Then we got fanciful: Pied Piper, Rodentia, Rat-a-tat-tat. Finally, we sank to the level of the absurd: Ratkill, Rat-Bomb, Rat-Shot. But all the names were inappropriate, or they couldn't be registered as a trademark, or they were in violation of an already existing trademark. So after great thought, and for the sake of expediency, we came up with the name d-Con, short for "decontaminate." It was a terrible name and we had every intention of changing it as soon as we could think of another one.

But we wanted to get the product out, and we had been wasting time. So d-Con it was. I spent a great deal of time and effort coming up with the copy that would sell the rat killer to the world. We put the spot on the air, but no one bought d-Con! We experimented with different stations and different copy approaches without luck. Apparently people weren't as ready for rat genocide as they were for fly genocide.

I explained this to Ratner and told him we should cut our losses and run.

"We can't do that," Ratner said.

"Why not?"

"Because I got a carload of warfarin, thirty-two thousand dollars of the stuff, and I got to get rid of it."

So he didn't let me rest. Instead, we took to the road.

Ratner and I got in his car and drove to downstate Illinois, looking for farmers to talk to. We called on the county agent, who gave us the names of many farmers he knew who had barns infested with rats. We wanted to talk to the farmers and see why they weren't buying the one product that could eliminate their problem.

But when we asked these farmers about their rodent problem, they looked at us as if we had asked them about the weather on Jupiter. They didn't have rats, they explained. Whatever gave us that idea, they wondered. They were afraid we were there to condemn their corn and grain for containing rat droppings.

When we introduced ourselves as representatives of the Wisconsin Alumni Research Foundation and explained that we were collecting data for a study on pest control, their attitude suddenly changed. For days, we heard rat story after rat story. They talked to us like a neurotic to his psychiatrist. They confessed that they were actually embarrassed about their rats; that rats were a stigma, connoting uncleanliness. Yes, they said, they would do anything to get rid of those rats, as long as no one knew about it. They made it clear they didn't want their neighbors or the postman to know they had a rat problem.

So we returned to Chicago and simply added one single line to our commercial: "So that no one will know you have a rodent problem, d-Con is always mailed in a plain wrapper." The commercial aired, and farmers across the country mailed in their orders.

In late 1949, you couldn't turn on the radio without hearing a spot for d-Con in the early morning hours or late at night. Through trial and error, we discovered we received the greatest response not during prime time but in those "off" hours. Virtually every 50,000-watt station in Mexico and the United States carried the d-Con message to people who were either getting out of bed or getting into bed. We were also on the "National Barn Dance," "Grand Ole Opry," "Louisiana Hayride," and "Arkansas Jamboree." All CBS stations carried "Housewife Protective League" (HPL);

in Chicago, it was Paul Gibson; Earl Nightengale had a similar show in Chicago. All pulled gung ho. This strange "off-hour" buying pattern was something I filed in the back of my mind for later use.

In the meantime, we were trying unorthodox methods of promoting d-Con. One involved the town of Middleton, Wisconsin, which served as the garbage dump for Madison. As a result, the streets of that city had been taken over by rats. People were afraid to go out after dark because of the severity of the problem. It was a citizen's nightmare and a rat killer's dream. In a joint project with the Wisconsin Alumni Research Foundation, we spread d-Con throughout the city. Thirty days later, we had wiped out the rat population in Middleton. Reader's Digest magazine gave the experiment a feature story, and we were off and running through Paul de Kruif, a contributor of science articles.

The Wisconsin Alumni Research Foundation also tested warfarin to see how it would affect farm animals. For instance, chickens were fed doses of d-Con over a long period of time without any adverse effect. The fact that d-Con was safe to use around farm animals certainly was a selling point. These test results and the Middleton story were incorporated into our commercials.

Soon, d-Con had transcended its function as a product. It had become a national "buzz" word. Whenever a product becomes something for disc jockeys and talk show hosts to use for a laugh, you know you've hit the big time. One disc jockey, Paul Faber, refused to read our commercial as it was written. Instead, his patter went something like, "I'd like to tell you how safe this d-Con is. They've fed enough d-Con to a chicken to kill nine thousand rats. And you know something? They took the dead chicken to a veterinarian, he did an autopsy, and when he opened up that chicken he said, 'Why, there ain't nothin' wrong with this here dead chicken.' "

It soon became obvious that d-Con had to expand out of the mail-order category into retail. We had received numerous requests from store owners to stock our product. But Ratner, as stubborn a man as I've ever met, refused. He said he didn't know anything about retail. We argued constantly, and finally he gave in. But he gave in in a way only Lee Ratner could: grudgingly. I had told Ratner that I knew a guy who ran a drugstore in Princeton, Illinois, who had promised four customers packages of d-Con. He offered to pay full retail if I would send them to him. When I told Ratner about this, he said, "You wanna go into retail? Okay, we'll go into retail. Send that guy a hundred forty-four packages and we'll see what happens." After suggesting that the whole idea bordered on insanity, I did what Ratner told me to do. When I informed the drugstore owner of what he should expect, he screamed, "A hundred forty-four packages! I don't sell a hundred forty-four tubes of toothpaste in a month. How am I going to get rid of a hundred forty-four packages of your goddamn rat poison?" "Try it," I said. "If you don't sell them, you don't have to pay for them."

Four days later, he called me up asking for another 288 packages. Apparently, it was the best-selling item his store had ever stocked.

About this time, a new marketing method was evolving. Products started as mail-order items, fostered consumer demand, and broke down the resistance of distributors to stock the product. Toni home permanent; a weight-reducer called Kyron; the Penman, a ball-point pen company, and Imdrin for arthritic pain were among the first to use this method. It became a very profitable way for smaller companies to break into the retail market.

We used this method to make d-Con a retail product. Ratner's resistance was eventually broken when McKesson & Robbins sent in a $50,000 order for d-Con.

Because d-Con is more Lee Ratner's story than mine, I feel compelled to end this chapter with the quintessential Ratner story. Its moral is simply that entrepreneurs dare go where fools fear to tread.

When d-Con was enjoying such fabulous success, Ratner was invited to a party on the yacht of Les Atlass, midwest vice-president of CBS and general manager of WBBM in Chicago. After one of those parties, Ratner called me and proudly proclaimed, "I just purchased fifteen minutes across the board from five forty-five to six A.M. on WBBM for eighteen hundred dollars. It's going to be a live talent show."

Steam was shooting out of my ears. He could have had live rats backing Mickey Mouse in a chorus of Handel's "Messiah" and nobody would have listened to the show at that early hour. I told him this in somewhat stronger language. When logic failed him, he used his old reliable final argument, "It's my money!"

I stopped worrying and Ratner started. We were losing our shirts on the buy. In his own inimitable fashion, Ratner called me and said, "Al, go over to Atlass and cancel this contract." I told him Atlass wouldn't cancel a firm contract for his own mother.

So Ratner decided to see Atlass on his boat, and negotiated a new deal. The next morning, I asked him if he had canceled the contract.

"Not exactly," he said.

"What do you mean, 'not exactly,' " I asked, wanting to hear what "not exactly" meant.

"Well, he traded us an hour on Saturday nights, using the same live talent, for the same price as before."

That sounded good to me. I asked to see the contract. Looking it over, I saw buried in fine print the stipulation that the show would run for a firm thirteen more weeks. I asked Ratner if he knew that he had bought a new thirteen-week schedule.

He didn't know. And then he turned a glowing red, sputtered and stuttered like a man possessed, grabbed me by the arm and shouted, "We're goin' to see Atlass."

We went over to the Wrigley Building, rushed past the startled WBBM receptionist, whizzed by Atlass's private secretary, and burst into Les's office. Ratner, with a look in his eye generally reserved for rats and flies, looked at Atlass and hissed, "Les, I don't mind when I get screwed, but when I get screwed, I like to get kissed."

Atlass calmly pushed a button on his desk. His secretary entered. Atlass looked up at her and nonchalantly remarked, "Kiss him!"

2

Never Buy
a Larry Joint
from a Pitchman

Eventually, Lee Ratner made me an offer I couldn't refuse and I became advertising manager of d-Con. I was given carte blanche to lead the company wherever I thought there was money to be made. In 1950, I led the company into a revolutionary approach to advertising. Many advertisers didn't think much of it then; it was primitive, a passing fancy, and reached a very limited audience. Still, I thought television advertising might have a future.

I thought that after seeing one of the first thirty-minute, "direct-response" television commercials. It was for Vita Mix, a blender that sold for $29.95. I called up the telephone-answering service that monitored requests for the product, and they told me they had received 325 phone calls. Factoring in the additional product orders they would receive by mail, I calculated that the commercial sold 500 units of Vita Mix, which translates into $15,000 worth of business.

I was astounded. It was like someone had shown me land with a billion gallons of oil underneath it and handed me a drill. With the right products, I knew we could make millions. It wasn't difficult to convince Ratner of this. For all his idiosyncracies, Ratner was as astute a businessman as ever walked the earth. So we began our foray into videoland with this question: How do we find products suitable for the medium?

Thinking about the problem, a solution immediately came to mind: the pitchmen.

We decided they had the products and the pitches to make television the most effective selling tool in the history of mankind. How we brought the pitchmen onto the small screen will be discussed in the next chapter. First, I must explain who the pitchmen were and how they happened to possess perfect pitch. Even in the fifties, pitchmen were a dying breed. Once they roamed the land free and easy as you please, their traveling medicine shows visiting a town as regular as clockwork. They had the gift of gab and could charm ten-dollar bills out of the most tightfisted of men. Their razzle-dazzle sales pitches were an art form; they would demonstrate how a product worked with flair and grace, and everyone from hicks to high-rollers would fall under their spell.

But times changed, and the pitchmen became traveling salesmen, loaded down with corporate baggage: rules and regulations watered down their approach. The company told them what to sell and how to sell it, and the magnificent selling techniques of the old pitchmen all but disappeared. (Today, of course, the pitchman has evolved into the "spokesperson.")

Still, a few stubborn souls refused to give in to those changing times. In 1950, you could still find a pitchman at a state fair or carnival or trade show, drawing a crowd with his pitch sure as a magnet draws metal. They sold anything and everything: an ordinary product could be magically transformed by an extraordinary pitch. Vitamins became miracle drugs, and a simple tool became a technological breakthrough.

The pitchmen were characters out of Dickens, speaking a language as exotic as that of a Cockney street vendor and as fiendishly clever as Fagin. They were true Gypsies, at home only when they were on the road, and they lived to sell.

Pitchmen had a vocabulary all their own. Once, I was driving with a pitchman and we were looking for a place to eat. I saw a place called Jim's Diner and suggested we stop there. He said, "That's a Larry." "No," I said, "that's Jim's." He then explained that "Larry" referred to anything bad. Apparently, in the mythology of pitchmen, there once lived a huckster named Larry Goldstein. He couldn't sell a good product to save his life. But give him a schlocky one of absolutely no value and he could sell millions. Therefore, when a pitchman heard about a bad product, he'd say, "That's one for Larry." Over the years, "Larry" became a generic term for anything that was lousy.

A conversation between two pitchmen might go something like this: "That was a real Larry joint, huh?" "You know it. Short lines all the way down the road." "Yeah, I've had some pretty good tips here and there, but not too many mooches." That conversation makes sense once you realize that "joints" mean products, "lines" mean money, "tips" refer to the crowd, and a "mooch" is an individual buyer.

A pitchman would begin his pitch with a "holder" and "flash." The holder was simply a device to keep the audience listening, and the flash were props used in the holder. Flash included snakes, dyed hamsters, guinea pigs, scantily clad women, and Indians.

Art Nelson, a legendary pitchman, had a great "holding" technique. He actually embarrassed his tips into listening to him. That master of palaver would fix his tip with a challenging stare and declare, "Anyone who thinks he's so smart there's nothing more to learn, get outa here." Those who had started to drift away would freeze. He continued: "But if you're smart enough to know that there's something new to learn every day, stick around. Because I'm going to tell you something that could affect the rest of your lives."

And then there was Frenchy Bordeaux. Like any self-respecting Frenchman, he believed in flamboyant gestures. One of the most flamboyant holders began with Frenchy demanding everyone take their wallets out of their pockets and hold them in their hands. Then, with great Gallic anger in his voice, he would proclaim, "Ladies and gentlemen, there is a pickpocket in your midst." With an actor's gift, he would stare into the audience as if he were talking to the guilty party, and say, "I don't know if you're here to buy or to steal, but I had you arrested once and I want you to get out. If you don't leave in five minutes, I'll call the police." Of course, no one would leave. Far better to serve a fifteen-minute audience sentence listening to Frenchy's pitch than to leave and feel a hundred eyes branding you a guilty man.

Those pitchmen were obsessed. Their obsession was selling, and nothing else mattered. It was not so much the money that was their raison d'être but the actual process of making the sale. Anyone or anything that got in the way had better beware. Once, I was at a Toronto fair, and the main attraction was Marilyn Bell attempting to swim from the New York shore to the Canadian shore. The fairground was empty and the beach was filled with spectators. The swimmer was only three miles from shore. As I walked through the midway, I passed a pitchman who looked forlorn. I asked him why he wasn't watching the swimmer approach. With pure vehemence, he hissed, "That son-of-a-bitch should have drowned hours ago."

Pitchmen never had money. Even though many of them made a thousand dollars or more a week, they seemed to spend the money faster than they made it. They subscribed to the philosophy of "Live fast, die fast, and have a good-looking corpse." Today, everyone talks about "creativity" in advertising, referring to the clever puns and visual images sprinkled throughout ads. Yet the creativity I believe in—and that the pitchman mastered—was the creativity involved in selling a product. He put a large part of himself into every pitch, summoning every resource he possessed to get a mooch. Like a mad poet, he got a crazed gleam in his eyes when he invented a holder and flash that knocked the tip for a loop.

There was a pitchman named Two-Faced Dempsey. He

was an expert mimic, the Rich Little of his era. I was on the road with him in Peoria when he hit upon a scheme for picking up a little spending money. We were in a Chinese restaurant, and as he eyed a tray of strange-looking Chinese candies, I could almost hear the whir of his pitchman's brain at work. He bought 150 pieces of candy for a dollar. He also bought a Chinese calendar and borrowed a small, tasseled silk hat. He next went to a drugstore and bought some makeup, which he put on his face. We then went to Peoria's open-air market. He tacked the Chinese calendar to a wall, squinted his eyes in such a manner that they gave the illusion of being almond-shaped, put on his silk hat, and started his pitch, speaking in a Chinese-accented voice. First, Dempsey explained that the calendar on the wall was his diploma from the University of Shanghai. Then, he told the growing crowd that the candy was Jismsan, an amazing sex pill.

"Why you think there eight hundred million Chinese, only two hundred million Americans?" Dempsey asked.

"Answer: Jismsan." Dempsey held the candy aloft, and a crowd of at least a hundred people gazed upon it wistfully.

"It is ancient Chinese secret, old as Confucius. I smuggled these out of the country. Would have been killed if caught. This Jismsan contain what you call stimulant, works within five minutes after taking.

"But be careful!" he warned the crowd, which by now looked like country boys at a big city strip show. "Never take a whole pill! You must cut it in half, for if you take a whole one your wife will never forgive you."

Dempsey proceeded to inform the crowd that the pills cost only "one dollar American." He added that it was not so much money, when you considered that one half pill lasted for twelve hours. The tip surged forward at the end of the pitch, and they bought all the "pills" he had. I would like to think that Peoria's growth as a town was due, in no small part, to Dempsey's Chinese pills.

Today, the pitchman is virtually extinct. It might seem that his death was a good thing. After all, he could easily be viewed as a charlatan and con man. But if you think that way, you are missing the point. As you shall see in the following chapters, much of what he sold was beneficial. And he possessed a genuine enthusiasm for the products he was selling. Many commercials today reek of phoniness. The viewer senses that the spokesperson is an actor or actress, not someone who truly believes in the product. The pitchman, for all his faults, conveyed a sense of excitement about a product, no matter what that product was. Each had an emotional investment in what he sold, and he tried his damndest to make that investment pay off.

And so I wondered, could the pitchman make the transition from a live appearance to television? Would his impact be diminished when confined to the tiny dimensions of a television screen? Would a pitch that worked for a hundred people work for thousands? I had doubts, but I also had faith. After all, if a Chinese sex pill played in Peoria, it would play anywhere.

3

The Thirty-Minute Commercial

Ratner and I found our first TV pitchman at a garden show in Chicago. His name was Bobby Green, and he was selling a knife sharpener/glass cutter. He had a good product and what we thought was a good pitch. We approached him and asked if he would like to be on TV. He had trouble visualizing what we were talking about. For a pitchman accustomed to working live crowds, a television commercial seemed like something out of science fiction. Still, when we started talking about money, we found a language he could understand. We asked him how much he made on an average day. He said five hundred dollars, which was obviously a lie. Still, we offered him five hundred if he would make a commercial for us, and also offered 5 percent of the sales the commercial generated. He agreed to do it.

Ratner and I assumed it would be easy. We rented a film studio, brought Bobby Green and his product in, turned the camera on him, and told him to do exactly what he did at Navy Pier except that he had to start out the commercial by saying, "My name is Bobby Green. I represent the Grant Company of Chicago." We didn't foresee the effect the

19

camera would have on him. With its beady eye staring Green in the face, he lost his pitchman's characteristic smoothness. In fact, it took him twenty-seven takes to get his first line right. He'd say, "My name is Bobby Green, and I represent the Chicago Company." Take two: "My name is Bobby Grant, and I represent the Green Company." Take a break. After two days of shooting, he finally got it right. It took so much time because of our insistence that the commercial be shot in one single take for the sake of credibility. Rather than using several cameras and cutting to close-ups to cut out mistakes, we decided to start from scratch whenever something went wrong. And, of course, it was extremely frustrating to film nine minutes of perfect pitch and suddenly have to start from the beginning when a mistake was made.

Still, we thought there was no other way to do it. Our potential customers were naturally wary of the new medium and a pitchman's speed. For them, television was magic, and it was difficult for people to believe what they were seeing. What we had to avoid at all costs was contributing to that aura of illusion. We needed to convey the quality of cinéma vérité for our commercials to be effective. Thus, it was imperative that the camera not waver from the pitchman. It had to look "live." If we allowed any quick cuts or jumpy edits, the viewer would reject the product instantly. It would appear that the pitchman was a magician not a salesman.

This decision paid off as the knife sharpener/glass cutter racked up incredible sales, moving almost 800,000 units at $2.98 in little more than a year. News of our success spread, and soon we were inundated with pitchmen and their products.

Then came food slicers, magic towels, chemical rug cleaners, chrome cleaners, fishing kits, tools, cooking pots, fly killers, gem setters, and the wonderfully named Blitz Hocker, a rotary chopper that revolved in a manner that facilitated the cutting of any food.

These pitchman presentations were the most perfect sales vehicles ever created. They were perfect because the pitchman had chopped, sliced, diced, and thrown away the parts of his presentation that didn't work. He had given the pitch to countless numbers of people all over the country. He'd test lines and discard those that didn't make the customer reach in his pocket. Bringing the pitchman commercial to television was like bringing a play to Broadway: you played the smaller towns and cities, constantly revising and rethinking the lines until they were just right. By the time the pitchman appeared on television, he knew exactly what to say, how to demonstrate his product, the tone of voice he should use, even the expression he should wear on his face. It was a perfect presentation because it had evolved to its highest form.

In the early days of television, the pitchman didn't have to compress his pitch into an arbitrary time limit. If the pitch took thirteen minutes, then the commercial was fifteen minutes with a two-minute tag. If it was twenty-five minutes, then the commercial was thirty minutes with a five-minute tag. (Today, of course, two-minute commercials are the longest allowed by the FCC and thirty-second spots are the rule.)

The pitchman commercials were elastic; they could easily be shaped and revised to fit any product. It would be a mistake, however, to think that all pitchman commercials were alike: they were as different from one another as a knife sharpener is from a Mixmaster blender. What they had in common was that they held a viewer's interest. In these times of thirty-second spots, in which information about a product is as hard to come by as water in a desert, it seems incredible that a product's features could be elucidated for up to thirty minutes. But that was precisely the point of the pitchman commercials: the product was allowed to sell itself. Of course, that meant we had to find products that were beneficial enough to justify ten to thirty minutes of air time. If a product wasn't unique, if it didn't offer a demonstrable consumer benefit, I crossed it off my list.

Let me give you an example of a fifties' commercial composition. Each had a holder, a promise of something spectacular to come later, a promise of great value, a complete demonstration of the product, and finally, "the turn"—the part of the commercial when the pitchman usually began, "I'll tell ya what I'm gonna do," and then offered a number of free items as he asked for the money.

After a brief period of time, we developed a standard operating procedure for our commercials. After finding a pitchman and the product, we would do the commercial live and then wait for the orders. If there were a sufficient number of orders, only then would we film the commercial.

Much has been written about the perils of producing early television shows, but compared to the problems of producing a live commercial, they seem relatively simple. While those television shows had large crews and professional entertainers, we often used amateurs and flew by the seat of our pants. Murphy's law was in force: If something can go wrong, it will go wrong. I approached each live commercial with a mixture of anticipation and trepidation.

Never will I forget the commercial we shot for a food slicer at WTTV in Indianapolis. A live band concert was on the air. Once the concert was over, we had thirty seconds to move the band out of the studio and set up our commercial. Behind the band was a curtain. Behind the curtain, with two feet of clearance, was a refrigerator with all the vegetables and fruit we would need for our pitch. I also was behind the curtain, ready to run out with the fruit and vegetables to the table as soon as the concert was over. As the band began their last number, "Stars and Stripes Forever," I opened the refrigerator. To my utter chagrin, oranges, apples, and tomatoes began spilling out, rolling among the members of the band. Instinctively, I crawled under the curtain on my hands and knees among the band members as "Stars and Stripes Forever" blared above me. The director got excited, hit the long-shot button, and caught all the action.

But that miscue was minor compared to the one that occurred at a station in South Bend, Indiana. It was a live commercial for a blender. During the commercial, the pitchman would grind a variety of ingredients in the blender, pour the concoction into a glass, toast the viewers, and drink it. Everything was going along smoothly until the pitchman realized that no one had put a glass on the table for him to use. Undaunted, he ad-libbed that he would get a glass from a cabinet behind him. Unfortunately, he didn't realize that the cabinets weren't real but were simply painted replicas of a kitchen on framed canvas. As he walked toward the fake cabinet, we frantically signaled for him to stop. He mistook our gesturing as a signal to hurry. So he hurried to the cabinet, grabbed the fake handle, yanked, and the entire backdrop tumbled on him.

Like the phoenix, he rose from the debris. And as only a true pitchman could, he recovered his composure and continued his presentation as if nothing had happened. In a calm, smooth tone, he explained, "Of course, there was supposed to be a glass here on the set, but as there is no glass, may I toast you by drinking directly from the blender bowl." With that, he raised the bowl to his lips and poured the drink into his mouth. He also poured it onto his clothes. Pieces of celery, radishes, and carrots that had not been fully liquefied clung to his tie and jacket. A three-inch piece of celery hung stubbornly to his upper lip and bobbed up and down as he continued to speak. It was a disaster for us, but more of a disaster for him as his 5 percent went down the drain.

But none of these incidents can compare with the "Hot Bed of Coals" snafu.

It began with a product called Kool Foot Oil. The product was guaranteed to ease the pain of tired, aching feet. To graphically illustrate the product's benefits—and to have an effective audience holder—I came up with a show-stopping idea for a live commercial: get a professional swami to walk across a bed of red-hot coals and then rub the Kool Foot Oil on his feet, thus demonstrating its efficacy.

I called a variety of talent agencies, looking for someone who could perform the stunt. After much searching, we finally found someone who claimed he could do it.

The talent arrived in the studio about thirty minutes before the commercial was to air. We dressed him in a sultan's outfit, attempting to give him the look of a swami. It was then that I noticed that our "swami" was sweating profusely. I asked him what was wrong.

"Well," he said, staring at the smoking coals in the studio. "I guess I'm a little nervous."

"Why?" I asked. "You've certainly done this before."

"Yeah," he said, "I guess I was exaggerating."

"Well, how many times have you done it?"

"Uh, I haven't really ever done it before."

"What!" I yelled, knowing the cameras were starting to roll.

"But I know how to do it. You just have to soak your feet in brine for three days before you do it."

"Oh," I said, relieved.

"Yeah, but you see, I just found that out yesterday."

"What?" I shouted. At this point he was going to walk the coals if it burned off both his feet.

But he was spared that fate when I came up with another idea. Calling it the "Red Sea Effect," I instructed the studio propmen to make a path through the middle of the coals. By positioning the camera correctly, we could create the illusion that he was actually walking on top of the coals. The commercial would be saved.

A few minutes later, the commercial began. Our swami started his journey through the flaming, hissing coals, and the effect was spectacular. And it became even more spectacular when the swami's silk pantaloons suddenly burst into flames. We were able to save the swami but not the commercial.

Perhaps the best thing about the pitchman commercials was the aura of excitement that surrounded the initial test. Testing a live commercial was like testing a new lure in a lake stocked with fish; the anticipation preceding the strike was tremendous. You knew the audience was there, but you were never quite sure how they would react.

In those early days of television, we discovered some highly successful products. In fact, many of the pitchman's products were the prototypes of even more successful products manufactured by major corporations today. For instance, we developed a product we called the Robot Gardener. It was simply a hose attachment, which you loaded with fertilizer, weed killer, or insecticide pellets, and it combined with the water to effectively and easily spray an entire lawn. In various forms and manufactured by various companies, it is found on the shelves of virtually every hardware store in the country today.

Many other "modern" products have their roots in the pitchman era. One of the most useful and amazing products I ever encountered was Power Bond. It was basically the same as Krazy Glue and Super Glue, and it sold for $2.98. The product was ideally suited to the pitchman approach, its incredible binding power making it perfect for demonstrations.

The Salad Maker was the forerunner of La Machine and other electric salad-making devices that do exactly the same thing as our Mouli Salad Maker except that they work electrically instead of manually. (I still prefer the manual salad makers because you can better control the amount of chopping and grinding.)

In the early days of television, people did not have the antipathy toward advertising that they do today. In fact, many people looked forward to seeing a commercial. This was because the commercial actually gave them information about a product, not a song and a dance. Like the Sears catalog years ago, TV opened up a whole new world of useful, innovative product presentations to viewers. The excitement generated by the pitchman's demonstration kept them glued to their seats. As a testament to the power of these commercials and their ten- to thirty-minute lengths, they were often listed in the TV guides as programs. People would look in the TV guides to discover the Salad Maker was running from 11 to 11:10 P.M. or that the Shining Knight commercial was at midnight. I once saw a letter from WGR-Buffalo written to A. C. Nielsen: "Please check your ratings for the week of April 7 through April 14. It might interest you to know that the Salad Maker commercial, which we have been running for two years, has a higher rating than the "Lawrence Welk Show."

Perhaps the most popular commercial of this era was the Charles Antell lanolin pitch. Lanolin was claimed to prevent hair loss. The pitchmen were Ricky Lewellyn and Charlie Kashir, and they were the dynamic duo of early fifties' advertising. You could hardly turn on a TV set in 1949–1951 without seeing their thirty-minute commercial. Lewellyn, with his bountiful head of hair, and Kashir, who was nearly bald, worked customers over like two cops; one with the hard sell and one with the soft sell. They began one of their pitches with a perfectly logical question: "Have you ever seen a bald-headed sheep?" They then explained that no one ever had because sheep had an ingredient in their wool called lanolin, which prevented hair loss. For any man or woman who cringed at the thought of losing hair, their pitch was easy to buy. So easy, in fact, that they sold millions of bottles of Charles Antell lanolin.

By today's standards, these commercials appear outrageous, unsophisticated, and unprofessional. But it was precisely the illogical rationale and the straightforward approach that sold products like nothing before or since.

I will never forget the opening line for a multivitamin pitchman commercial. It began with a simple statement: "The reason pigs win blue ribbons and people don't is that pigs get all the nutritious and vitamin-filled foods and people eat the garbage." It then explained how people could get the vitamins if they ate the peelings and skins. A bizarre approach? Perhaps. An effective one? The explosion of the multivitamin market that followed was due, in no small part, to the rationale of that commercial.

Imagine yourself sitting in front of a new television set, your attitude toward commercials much different than it is in the 1980s. You don't view them with disdain, automatically tuning them out when they interrupt your favorite program. Instead, you view them as a valuable source of information, as something with the potential to both sell and educate. As you're sitting there, you see a man standing beside a desk, and he says, "Don't touch that dial! Because the next few minutes could be the most important minutes of your life. What you're about to see and hear could very well start you on the road to a newfound happiness. . . greater success than you ever dreamed possible . . . income beyond your wildest imagination. Ladies and gentlemen, how would you like to have a push-button memory?"

Now let me interrupt this commercial for a question: Who among you is not intrigued by what is taking place on the television set? Unlike any commercial you might see today, it makes you want to continue watching because you're curious about the product. What is a "push-button memory"?

"How would you like to be able to remember first and last names of everyone you meet. I mean, every time you're introduced to a new person, you'll remember that person's name automatically, so if you meet again in a year—or five years—that person's name would pop into your memory automatically. Well, tonight you're going to get some memory tricks and formulas from Mr. Harry Lorayne . . . Mr. Lorayne's fantastic memory is not due to a photographic mind, but rather to a series of memory tricks, or formulas, which he has been able to teach to anyone in a few short hours."

The commercial then showed Harry Lorayne at work, demonstrating his amazing memory. The demonstrations were fascinating and convincing, and the viewer—like anyone witnessing what seems to be magic—wanted to know how the tricks were done. At that point, Lorayne introduced the product: a book called "How to Develop a Super-Power Memory."

He ended the commercial with the offer, explaining how to order the book. In any direct-response commercial, this is the crucial point, where you make the sale. The key to making the sale is to make it as easy as possible for the viewer to order. The spokesman must make ordering the product a logical, natural process. Everything in the commercial has been leading up to the close: if exactly the right words aren't used, you've blown it. Here is how Harry Lorayne ended his pitch:

"If 'How to Develop a Super-Power Memory' doesn't teach you how to remember names, faces, numbers, events, facts, and ideas, if you don't startle your friends and employees with fantastic new super memory, if all facts, names, and figures aren't embedded in your mind so you'll never forget, then this book costs you absolutely nothing. Remember, you don't have to study this book. You don't have to give me months, weeks, even days. Give me one night! Now here's how to get your copy of 'How to Develop a Super-Power Memory' on a no-risk, free-trial offer."

One of the most successful and outrageous commercials of the pitchman era was the one for Vita Mix. The commercial ran for thirty minutes and virtually deified the Vita Mix machine. It was pure pitchman all the way, pulling out all the stops to convince people that Vita Mix was the greatest kitchen aid since the stove. On paper, perhaps it seems a little ridiculous, but when it aired, it was an irresistible presentation that appealed to every woman with a hungry family to feed. I have used the basic elements of the commercial—if not the style—throughout my advertising career. Those elements can be roughly defined this way: tease 'em, please 'em, seize 'em. Or, if you prefer acronyms, TPS. You tease the viewer by raising his expectations. You promise the viewer a product that is better and more useful than anything he's ever seen. You please him with the demonstration of the product: a demonstration that has an almost visceral fascination. And, finally, you seize him with the offer: an offer so attractive, ordering the product seems like a perfectly logical thing to do.

4

FOR SALE:
Beautiful Florida
Retirement Sites
(Alligators Included
at No Extra Charge)

Fortunes were made during the early days of TV. Those who became fabulously wealthy were the wheelers and dealers. They didn't spot trends; they started them. Anything that had profit written all over it was fair game.

In the early fifties, there were very few rules governing what could and could not be advertised on television, and how it could be advertised. Thus, the idea of selling retirement land in Florida seemed to be an opportunity waiting to be seized.

Lee Ratner had thirty thousand acres of land in Florida that he didn't know what to do with. The land was in the middle of the Everglades, and Ratner originally ran it as a cattle ranch. But he encountered a variety of problems, and after taking losses on his ranch for five years, his attorneys advised him to change the designation of the land so he could continue to take tax write-offs. Thus, he decided to turn the land into retirement sites and sell them on television using the name Lehigh Acres.

Nothing like this had ever been done before. As with most of Ratner's programs, there was always a high-risk ele-

29

ment. Most of Ratner's land was covered with water and infested with snakes, alligators, and mosquitos, but Ratner decided to sell the land at a reasonable price and ultimately put in drains, roads, and the necessary improvements. (Unlike many of the developers who would follow Ratner's lead, he was honest and offered consumers an excellent deal.) The price was set at $299 for a half-acre on a $10-down, $10-a-month financing plan with no interest. We decided to give it a try on TV. I figured if you could sell Florida sunshine somebody would buy it.

Creating a "pitchman-type" commercial for an intangible product was both a challenge and a test. How would people respond to the offer? Was it possible to stimulate inquiries through a television commercial and then send a second-step mailing piece to convert inquiries to sales?

We decided the key to the commercial's success was to treat Lehigh Acres like the Garden of Eden. If we could tempt the viewer with forbidden fruit, we would have him eating out of our hand. The question was: How to make the intangible tangible? For obvious reasons, we couldn't show pictures of the sites. A picture of an alligator sunning himself in the swamp would not create the proper atmosphere.

But what if we showed the benefits of Florida? What if we tantalized the viewer with pictures of orange groves and sandy beaches, sailboats and palm trees? What if we sold health, happiness, and peace of mind? And what if we offered all this at $10-down, $10-a-month? It was an irresistible offer. Motivating a TV viewer to act is an extremely difficult task, and it is made even more difficult when you are offering something he can't hold in his hand. But our concept was foolproof: An offer of paradise for $10 would trigger the buying impulse in any person approaching retirement age.

Generally, the best commercials are structured so that they gradually build in intensity. There is a logical progression from one product benefit to the next, a subtle increase in pressure on the viewer to act. I cannot put too much emphasis on how important it is not to peak too early in a commercial: If you load the first part of the spot with all the ammunition, everything that comes after it becomes anti-climactic and you've lost the viewer. It all goes back to the TPS formula: tease 'em, please 'em, and seize 'em. That is exactly what we did in the commercial for Lehigh Acres.

The commercial opened with a slide of a cabin cruiser and the announcer intoning: "Now is the right time to plan for those future retirement years when our children are grown, when we are no longer able to put in a strenuous day's work. When winter months aggravate all those ills caused by cold, damp climates." Flashing on the screen was a woman struggling through the wind and snow.

". . . How would you like to retire like a millionaire within a leisurely drive of the picturesque Floridian shores of the Gulf of Mexico. . . . Have juicy Florida oranges, grape-fruit, and those gracious palm trees right in your own back-yard? How would you like to fish, bathe, hunt, and sail? . . ."

You get the idea. Those questions were the "tease." You'll notice that no hard information about the offer has been given yet. So far, everything has been foreplay. Only when you're sure that you've hooked the viewer do you enter into the "please" phase of the pitch.

"Well, whether your income is thirty-five hundred dol-lars or ninety-five hundred a year, this future can be yours. And more important, you can afford it. Listen! For just ten dollars down—yes, I said ten dollars down and ten dollars a month—you can own a homesite of your own that measures a full one hundred and four feet by one hundred and four feet. An excellent high, dry tract in a retirement dreamland—Lehigh Acres, Florida."

After another minute of "please"—descriptions of Le-high Acres and what it had to offer—the commercial "seized" the viewer with specific information about how to obtain the Lehigh Acres brochure. "Lehigh Acres offers you the health, happiness, and peace of mind you've dreamed of . . . This information folder will be sent absolutely free without obligation. So act now while this property is still available. Here's your announcer who will tell you how to send for your colorful folder."

The commercial worked. Thousands of viewers wrote in

for the sales brochure and immediately sent in their $10 downpayment for their place in the sun. It was the first national land offer commercial following World War II and the first one ever on TV. Ratner had no intentions of bilking his customers, and he immediately began the process of putting in roads, power, and sewage-disposal facilities.

It had the potential to be one of the biggest money-making concepts of all time, but it worked so well that many shady operators soon entered the business. News of Lehigh Acres' success traveled fast, and it was not long before every two-bit con artist in America began selling swampland to unsuspecting customers. In the next few years, there were at least fourteen hundred different companies offering land in Florida, Arizona, and New Mexico. Less than three hundred offers were legitimate. Most companies had no intention of making the sites inhabitable.

Exposés of "land fraud" were headlined in papers throughout the country, and the public began to mistrust all land offers. Soon it became necessary for Florida to lay down a complex series of laws and regulations for land sellers to follow, and to conform to these regulations we were forced to raise prices of a half-acre to more than five times the original asking price.

Still, we were able to make a decent profit on Lehigh Acres and other land development projects we advertised. In fact, anyone who bought one of our sites and moved into the area literally found themselves the most pampered tenants on Earth! Enormous golf courses and elaborate recreational facilities were constructed for thousands of people, yet only a few were there to use the facilities. People who bought the first lots found themselves enjoying country clubs, organized recreation, pools, gyms, boating facilities, and a complete staff of service people whose only job was to keep the residents happy so they would recommend the area to potential buyers who came to look at the sites.

In some cases, the key to a successful development was as simple as being able to provide residents with adequate water. Because many of the sites in Arizona, New

Mexico, and Texas were located in arid and semiarid areas, water shortage was the major problem many developers encountered. There is the story of the El Paso developer who had spent enormous amounts of money buying up land and found himself without a sufficient supply of water. He immediately invested in drilling equipment to explore for a water source. One day, one of his drillers rushed into his office and excitedly told him they had hit natural gas. The developer screamed, "To hell with the gas. We need water, keep drilling!"

5

I Love Lucy, but I Wouldn't Let My Products Appear on Her Show

For a long time, the ratings problem had bothered me. Even during my radio years, I had noticed that there was often no correlation between a show's ratings and the results or orders it pulled for a product. Poorly rated shows would pull a larger number of orders, and high-rated shows would pull fewer orders. Yet everyone insisted that ratings were a logical way to buy time.

Logic, however, is a funny thing. Once upon a time, it seemed logical that no one could go faster than the speed of sound; that certain diseases had no cure; that the world was flat. Time, and the enterprising efforts of a few individuals, demonstrated that these "realities" were merely appearances.

So it was in the late fifties when I decided to explore the "reality" of ratings versus results. I compared shows with similar demographics—situation comedies with situation comedies, cowboy shows with cowboy shows. I compared results from the higher-rated shows against the lower-rated ones. My findings: in nearly every case, the studies demonstrated that lower-rated shows actually outpulled higher-rated shows in "direct-response" orders.

Even more surprising, placing a direct-response commercial on television's top-rated shows—"I Love Lucy," the

"Milton Berle Show"—was like assigning it to a cell in death row. Virtually no one ordered products advertised on those shows, despite the huge audiences. I also graphed the time of the day and days of the week when products sold best, and ultimately a pattern emerged: weekends, late at night, and early in the morning were the most effective hours for direct response.

Our research contradicted everything the advertising community preached and practiced. If the research held up, it would mean that there was a potentially revolutionary alternative to the standard media-buying methods; that you could kiss the premium prices for high-rated prime-time shows good-bye and concentrate your buys in optimum buying periods for a fraction of the usual cost.

To test the validity of my research, I contacted a highly respected professor at Northwestern University's Department of Industrial Psychology. I explained my findings and asked him if they made any sense. After studying the data I had collected and doing some research of his own, he posited a theory that put my findings into a psychological context. He began by telling me that all advertising is an attempt to get a prospective customer to act—to call a number, mail a letter, go to a store and buy a product. For advertising to be most successful, you have to reach the subject when he is most receptive and least likely to resist the advertiser's message. The professor explained that it is easiest to reach a person when he is most relaxed, most tired, and has the fewest outside distractions. This occurs when he first gets up, before he goes to bed, and on weekends. He builds up and lets down sales resistance on a daily basis as well as a weekly one. The curve looks like a seven-fingered hand.

The professor then added the clincher! He said that if you are trying to reach a potential customer, the worst time to do it is during a popular prime-time show. While watching that type of show, the viewer is fully alert and he resents the commercial interruption.

Within the context of our research and the professor's explanation, everything made perfect sense. Indeed, con-

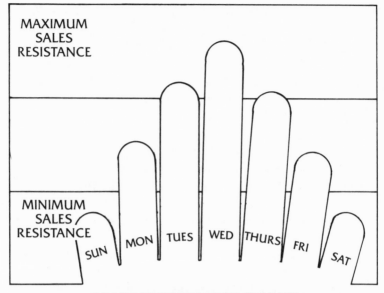

MAXIMUM
SALES
RESISTANCE

MINIMUM
SALES
RESISTANCE

SUN MON TUES WED THURS FRI SAT

SALES RESISTANCE CHART

trary to popular opinion, the world wasn't flat and prime time wasn't the best time.

Perhaps the easiest way to understand the sales-resistance theory is to picture someone watching "I Love Lucy." Let's call this someone Mrs. Buyer. Mrs. Buyer's favorite show is "I Love Lucy." She looks forward to it with great expectation after a hard day of washing the floors, making dinner, and putting the kids to bed. She watches Lucy and Ricky Ricardo and Fred and Ethel Mertz go through their routines with uncommon interest, totally immersing herself in their antics. So when a commercial interrupts the show, she cannot help but react negatively. For her, the show is an escape, and the commercial brings her back to the real world. To advertise a kitchen cleanser or laundry detergent is sheer madness, reminding Mrs. Buyer of something she is trying to forget.

Now imagine the same Mrs. Buyer watching an old movie before she goes to bed. She is watching the film with only half the interest with which she watched "I Love Lucy." In fact, she's half asleep. Mrs. Buyer has downshifted her mind into low gear, splicing in random thoughts with scenes from the movie. So when the commercial interrupts the film, she is not annoyed: she wasn't paying that much attention to the film, anyway. She is relaxed, and she does not reflexively block a commercial message. She is willing to stop, look, and listen to what is on the screen. If the commercial is good, it's as interesting as the movie! Mrs. Buyer is more willing to listen to the message than she was three hours ago. The demonstration of a useful, beneficial product has a visceral impact: "Yes," she thinks, "I really could use that blender." Reaching for the phone is a natural response: she is in a mood that predisposes her to phone in her order. In Mrs. Buyer's relaxed, receptive state, ordering a product by phone or mail seems a perfectly natural and easy response to the commercial's message.

I should note that my theory is less applicable to advertising that tries to gradually improve attitudes and awareness about a product and more applicable to advertising that tries to motivate a "decision to buy" before the commercial ends. Jingles like "Have a Coke and a smile" may get good results with high exposure and reach. That kind of advertising—some call it image or life-style advertising—can work during prime time. But it still runs the risk of what I call "negative recall," generating hostility toward the advertising for interrupting an interesting show.

From the moment I confirmed my suspicions about ratings, I eschewed prime time. Immediately thereafter, my agency began to grow by leaps and bounds and my clients' profits soared.

What was amazing to me was that others didn't tap this rich vein of viewers. Most advertisers seemed to believe that the poor ratings of non-prime-time shows rendered their commercials useless. To this day, many advertisers still believe that to be the case.

That, of course, is nonsense. Just look at the history of many products that, because of limited budgets, start off in fringe time. They establish distribution and a highly profitable advertising-to-sales ratio and then demand their agencies buy top-rated prime-time shows. Their advertising-to-sales ratios soar. They blame the marketing techniques, the com-

mercials, everything and everyone except the media department who is getting the "top prime spots" for them. This
has been the case with Alberto Culver, Lestoil, Miracle
White, and numerous other companies that forgot the old
saying: "Dance with the one who brung you to the dance."

The validity of the Theory of Sales Resistance would be
confirmed and reconfirmed many years after its conception in
1954. These confirmations would come from numerous and
varying sources, including other ad agencies conducting similar studies. One of the most interesting confirmations came
from Waseda University of Japan. They isolated a community
that delivered newspapers, periodicals, and mail at specific
times of the day and specific days of the week. They were then
able to actually measure the sales results attributed to the
various delivery times. Their findings as to periods of greatest
and least sales resistance were identical to ours.

(The confirmation of our theory of sales resistance—
using printed material instead of broadcast—also confirms
the reason why Sunday newspapers carry far more advertising than the weekday papers despite the tremendous competition of advertisers for the consumer dollar; and it
confirms why afternoon newspapers are unsuccessful. Advertisers tend to spend their money in the medium that delivers the best results. Because afternoon papers are read at
the wrong time, the afternoon paper gets a minimum of
advertising dollars. Because newspapers are bought as
much for the advertising as the editorial content, the lack of
advertising affects the circulation, causing the ultimate demise of the paper.)

Recent studies by several other major universities have
confirmed our theory through their studies of biorhythms.
According to these findings, everyone goes through biolog-
ical changes, which cause mental changes, which are cycli-
cal. The cycle a person is in at a given time determines how
that person will respond to a specific situation. During one
cycle, a person might say his favorite color is red. During
another one, he might say it's blue.

By extension, a person's biorhythms can determine how
he responds to a commercial. In one cycle, he might re-

spond positively; in another, negatively. Biorhythms, then, provide one explanation of why viewers are less resistant to motivational advertising during certain times of the day and days of the week.

Perhaps the most authoritative validation of the theory of sales resistance is found in the Burke Study. (Burke is a highly respected research organization.) One of their findings was that viewers did not have different images of corporations that ran commercials on highly rated network shows as compared with lower-rated shows on independent stations. More important, the study showed that recall and sales motivation were higher when commercials were aired on late-evening independent stations as compared with prime-time network ones.

Despite these confirmations, some agencies still are skeptical about the theory of sales resistance. One reason for this skepticism is that agencies and advertisers have no reliable gauge to measure a commercial's immediate effect on sales. Advertisers generally assume a cause-and-effect relationship between advertising and sales. If sales go up, the commercial is effective; if sales go down, the commercial is ineffective. But because there are many other factors that can influence sales—distribution, merchandising, publicity—it is difficult for most advertisers to judge the immediate and actual motivational power of their commercials.

Thus, many advertisers mistakenly rely on recall scores and awards as a barometer of their commercials' success. I use the word "mistakenly" because awards are given to commercials for their entertainment value, not for their ability to sell. And according to a recently published Marschalk Company study, high recall can actually hurt a product's sales.

According to this study, recall can be either positive or negative. It states that ". . . a commercial that's liked (positive) can move 31 percent of its viewers to consider buying the endorsed brand over others in the category, and a disliked commercial (negative) can move 33 percent of its viewers to go out of their way to buy any other brand."

Though the Marschalk study establishes negative and

positive recall, it fails to take the results of the study far enough. It fails to recognize all the factors that can produce negative recall.

A recently completed Eicoff agency study, based on six years of research, concludes that negative recall can be caused by airing the commercial at the wrong time. According to our study, an astounding 75 percent of viewers surveyed responded negatively when commercials interrupted favorite prime-time shows. Respondents repeatedly explained this negative reaction by saying they resented the interruption.

Conversely, few viewers responded negatively to commercials that interrupted reruns. According to the study, viewers did not resent commercial interruptions during shows in which they had only a minimal involvement.

There have been numerous occasions when a client has come to our agency and said he was not interested in a "motivating" commercial but rather one that would achieve a high level of recall or product recognition. To those clients, I've always responded: "I will guarantee you the highest level of recall you've ever seen or I will pay for your entire campaign."

The clients, of course, all stare at me with dumbfounded expressions and ask how I can make such an offer.

To which I've always replied: "I will make a sixty-second commercial with an Indian pounding a tom-tom and repeating the name of the product every three beats. At the end of the sixty seconds people watching the commercial will have switched stations, thrown an ashtray at the TV, or called the station to protest this incredibly obnoxious commercial.

"But no one who sees the commercial will ever forget it."

Our unique, post-analytical research gave birth to a number of other important theories, which will be discussed in the following chapters. Of these theories, none was more instrumental in changing standard media-buying practices than the Isolation Factor theory. It will be discussed in chapter 11.

6

There's No Business Like Show Business

Most of the advertising community looks back at the sixties and fondly refers to it as "The Golden Age of TV Commercials." Nothing could be further from the truth. Those years were golden only in the most literal interpretation of the word "golden," in that advertisers began pouring ridiculous amounts of money into the creation of thirty-second extravaganzas.

Prior to 1960, long demonstation commercials were the rule rather than the exception. Many of these commercials featured products sold by pitchmen. Many major corporations were still looking at television with a wary eye, assessing its potential as a selling tool. Thus, the pre-1960 commercials did not reflect a major corporation's concern with image—they did not have to look like or be expensive productions. In addition, the pitchmen who advertised on television did not have the luxury of experimenting with different approaches in their commercials. Their budgets were drum-tight, and the straightforward approach was the only approach that was viable. To make a commercial that did not hammer home a product's benefits in the most direct manner was suicidal.

Even Texaco, sponsor of the high-rated "Milton Berle Show," used the pitchman technique to sell their products. Sid Stone, an ex-pitchman, began each Texaco commercial with "Tell ya what I'm gonna do," and the audience loved it.

But in the sixties, Newton Minow's "vast wasteland" policies forced the pitchmen off the air. With his vendetta against longer commercials, he ensured that television was no longer the gold mine it once was for the pitchman. But major corporations, encouraged by Minow's pronouncements about how he had "cleaned up" television and the rapidly increasing number of TV sets turning up in people's homes (and the introduction of color TV), soon embraced the new medium with open pocketbooks. The economy was strong, big business was making money, and television presented them with an opportunity to make even more. So they hired the biggest ad agencies and virtually gave them carte blanche to produce commercials.

By and large, the agencies were staffed by a new generation of creative minds. They rejected the pitchman style as old-fashioned and unbecoming an image-conscious Fortune 500 corporation. The creative departments of these agencies had little or no experience in selling. Rather, they were people who considered themselves writers and artists, whose priorities often were style over substance and whose objective was to add to their portfolios and thus improve their chances of getting better jobs at other agencies.

Out of this environment, Doyle Dane Bernbach arose. They instituted a precedent-setting advertising philosophy that spread like wildfire. Basically, the key to that philosophy was a shift away from the marketing and merchandising of a client's product. They were concerned primarily with the "creative" aspect of advertising: their job stopped once the commercial was on the air. And it was an extremely effective approach for nonpackaged goods. No one can challenge their success with Volkswagen and Avis.

But it is also no coincidence that they have had problems with many packaged goods accounts they've handled. Still, others in the ad business looked at Doyle Dane's Volkswagen success and tried to copy it. They applied that "creative" strategy across the board—any product was fair game, and many products were killed because of it. Agencies separated into two camps: the "creatives" and the "fundamentalists." Back then, J. Walter Thompson fell into the latter category, and their commercials retained the spirit of the pitchmen, if not the style. Their work for Kraft Foods epitomized this approach: the commercials demonstrated how to make a sandwich or salad with Kraft cheese. As a result, Kraft cheese sales soared, for the spots focused on the product's benefits and disdained the superfluous. They provided the viewer with the motivation to go to the refrigerator and make a cheese sandwich.

Stan Freberg also had an enormous effect on sixties' advertising when he created those hilarious commercials for Chun King and Contadina. People across the country hailed those commercials as the work of an advertising genius, and humor became the be-all and end-all of television advertising. Agencies competed with one another like comedians on a talk show, each trying to top the other with humor. Advertising operated on the insane notion that the funnier or more entertaining a commercial was, the better it would sell the product.

Advertising became a faddish industry. Humor reigned for a few years, and then star testimonials took its place. When the testimonials faded, song-and-dance numbers became popular. Commercials soon were ignoring the product entirely, neglecting features and benefits as well as the essential information such as what the product cost, what it did, and where you could purchase it. Instead, advertising entered what I like to call "The Show Biz Era." Agencies competed for star spokespersons more fiercely than the movie studios. An agency creative producer would crow "I signed Robert Young" and another creative producer would boast "Yeah, but I got Ed McMahon." The product was ignored, treated as a prop and nothing more.

There were some agencies, however, that put celebrities in their proper places. June Lockhart, star of "Lassie," did an excellent job of telling listeners why her family liked "Shake 'n Bake" for General Foods. Anna Maria Alberghetti was skillfully selected by Ogilvy & Mather to sell Good Seasons salad dressing. Of course, no one can dispute the fact that Jane Russell was the perfect choice for the "big girls" Playtex bras.

In my experience, agencies go wrong when they choose celebrities for their star value rather than because they are "natural" spokespersons for the products.

The show biz analogy is supported by the sudden advent of awards. From nowhere, advertising awards sprang up, almost as numerous as the commercials. Andys, Clios, and a hundred other Emmy spin-offs became the creative department's goal. Unfortunately, almost all of these awards were for "creativity" and not for sales. (The exception to this obsession with "creativity for creativity's sake" was the David Ogilvy Award. Apparently as fed up with the award syndrome as I was, Ogilvy established an in-house award to be "given every year to the people who create the campaign that has done the most to produce results for the client's service, product, or reputation.")

The logical question is: Why did companies allow this trend to continue? Why did a company that had spent millions of dollars on "creative" commercials that had a negative effect on sales futilely grasp at "creative" straws? The answer, quite simply, is that big business was caught up in the excitement of show biz advertising. Instead of relying on commercials that promoted their company's good, steady growth, they were willing to risk everything on one spin of the wheel for the big score.

A pitchman commercial was structured so that it motivated instantly. And, conversely, if the pitchman commercial didn't work, it caused a company to suffer only minor losses. On the other hand, a show biz commercial required enormous investments of capital: big-budget production, prime-time buys, and network exposure over an extended period of "investment spending" were mandatory. As a result, a company like Ballantine Beer switched to the "creative" approach and promptly dropped seven places in market position.

The product managers of big companies were—like their agency counterparts—a new breed. They were part of the "Ivy League" Syndrome. Fortune 500 companies started hiring product managers straight out of prestigious business schools. These scholar-businessmen had a vast knowledge of marketing equations and little knowledge of how a business actually worked. They misinterpreted the casebook study of Volkswagen and tried to apply it to their company's packaged goods product. And many of these product managers had never worked in a store or sold anything in their entire lives!

Their bosses bowed to their enthusiasm and education. They were swept up in the awards sweepstakes, as agency and client combined forces to get image-building Clios rather than product-building sales.

If you look at the major award winners of the sixties, you'll see how meaningless those awards really were. Let me quote an article from Advertising Age magazine that appeared July 10, 1967, discussing the Clio award winners:

> Without a doubt, this is the funniest reel of winners in all of television's history. . . . But the laughter has begun to die away, less than two months later, as the agencies that won four of the Clios have lost the accounts. Another Clio winner is out of business. Another Clio winner has taken its $5 million budget out of TV. Another has taken one-half of its brand's business to another shop. Another Clio winner refused to put its entry on the air. Two other are in serious jeopardy at this time.
>
> How long can this distorted sense of "creativity" go on? We checked back on the television "classics" picked by the festival for previous years. There's a total of 81. And 36 of the agencies involved have either lost the account or gone out of business.
>
> Could the kiss of Clio be the kiss of death?

But, of course, it was as Cole Porter said: "Anything goes." And everything did. Product spokespersons ceased to be living, breathing human beings. In their place were chipmunks, beavers, and talking hands. Animation was in vogue and you couldn't tell the Saturday morning cartoons from the commercials. Fantasy and sex grabbed the advertisers' imaginations, and commercials looked as if they were filmed by Fellini.

Now I don't want to give the impression that none of these commercials was effective. Some of them—especially the ones for similar products—created brand awareness that eventually boosted sales. But certain products succeeded in spite of their advertising, not because of it. If a company had a big enough advertising budget and a terrific distribution network, they could make a product sell no matter how ludicrous their advertising might be.

But there is no doubt that the "let-us-entertain-you" attitude toward advertising in the sixties made television advertising a less effective selling tool than it was in the fifties. It created an infrastructure that still dominates the business. Big ad agencies added massive research departments whose sole function was to churn out millions of pages of theoretical research. From this theoretical research, theoretical commercials would be made, and often the theory did not work outside of the laboratory.

This type of research is overstressed. No matter what questions are asked, the answers are always suspect. They are the victims of what psychologists call the Hawthorne Effect: in an experiment, the control's knowledge that he is part of an experiment taints the results. Similarly, when a researcher asks a consumer questions, the consumer often gives the answers he thinks the researcher wants to hear. For instance, if a car manufacturer is thinking of introducing a new car, he might ask certain questions to determine the public's receptivity to that car. So when the researcher asks a question such as "Would you consider buying an electric car?" the consumer would probably answer affirmatively, assuming that was the expected answer. Of course, this same person would probably never buy such a car. This type of research was responsible for one of the classic failures in American marketing: the Edsel.

There is the story, perhaps apocryphal, of a major New York agency that commissioned its research department to do extensive research for a client. The client, a soft drinks manufacturer, requested the agency research the public reaction to a new soda pop—one that had very few calories. This was before the diet drink revolution. Spending hundreds of thousands of dollars of the client's money on research, the agency concluded that people would never drink soda that wasn't chock-full of sugar; that they preferred everything from water to fruit juices over a diet drink. Theoretical research once again "triumphed" over good business sense.

Still, such failures didn't stop the trend toward theoretical research. Agencies had a great stake in continuing such research, particularly by outside research organizations, for not only did it bring in additional income but it could be used as a defense mechanism to justify advertising failure.

For instance, if a commercial bombed, the agency could simply point to their research and say, "We followed the research." And if the commercial worked, the research was never mentioned.

The rise in theoretical research led to the de-emphasis of the only research worth a damn: post-analytical research that determines advertising's actual effect on sales. In the sixties, the Eicoff agency regularly used post-analysis to determine a commercial's effect on sales in specific markets.

From analytical research in four or five test markets, we could discover if a commercial was generating enough sales to justify expanding advertising expenditures in other markets. If sales didn't justify expansion, the client had several choices: (1) reshoot the commercial, (2) reposition the product, (3) take the product out of distribution and keep losses at a minimum.

If, however, post-analytical research indicated sales were good, the client could expand into other markets. By

the mid-sixties, we had compiled what we termed a Product
Marketing Index (PMI) for every market in the country. Thus,
by gauging sales in specific test markets, sales could be projected for all markets. If, for instance, a commercial generated sales of 500 units of a product in two weeks in
Portland, it was possible to forecast sales to within 5 percent
in all major markets, big and small.

The exception to the PMI rule are products that are af-
fected by climate, ethnicity, regional customs, geographical
variables, or any conditions that are unique to that specific
market.

Using post-analytical research it is possible to keep initial advertising expenditures relatively small. For under
$10,000 in media, one could test a complete marketing
program, increasing that figure only if it was warranted by
sales. But on another level, the PMI allows one to control
the advertising-to-sales ratios on a market-by-market basis
just as the pitchman controlled his day-to-day expenditure.
Using this approach, one is not tied to trends, producing
fashionable commercials. Rather, commercials have only one
purpose: to generate sales. If a client doesn't get demonstrable proof that the commercial is working, he changes
commercials or fires the agency. This "put up or shut up"
approach was (and is) a trademark of our agency.

In the sixties, this method was viewed as paradoxical by
the industry. They wouldn't accept it for what it was: a viable
advertising/marketing strategy. Instead of utilizing the techniques we pioneered (theory of sales resistance, PMI, Key
Outlet Marketing, etc.), they remained mired in the muck of
show biz advertising. Hotshot "creative" types sneered
when A. Eicoff & Company was mentioned, referring to the
agency as the "King of the Late Night Pitchmen."

As the sixties flew by, the straightforward technique was
refined to meet the needs of a new generation of products
and advertisers. The time would soon come when major
corporations would grow weary of agencies that gave them
Clios and no sales.

7

Thank You,
Newton Minow

It could have been a disaster.

When Newton Minow took over the FCC in the early sixties, a shiver ran down the back of anyone involved in television direct-response advertising. He was a reformer, and with his power he could make life miserable for the Old Guard. It was similar to what happens when a liberal mayor is elected in a town dominated by machine politicians. The new mayor vows that he's going to clean up the town and "throw out the rascals." Of course, all that mayor does is put in his own rascals, and the old ones either adapt to the new regime or get out.

In Newton Minow's famous "vast wasteland" speech, which probably did more to hurt good TV programming than any single event in TV's history, he promised to clean up the airwaves. With that speech, he pounded the nails in the pitchman's coffin. He railed against the glut of ten-minute-and-longer commercials that "polluted" the medium. For Minow, direct marketing was a sleazy, disreputable business that had no place in the idealistic Kennedy era. Remember, this was the time of the "New Frontier," when moneymak-

ing entrepreneurs were frowned upon. (Ironically, that included Joseph P. Kennedy, who epitomized that type of
entrepreneur.) Minow's vision of television was one of cultural enrichment, free of the crass commercialization of the
fifties. Of course, this was upper-class snobbery and nothing
else. From his lofty perch, Minow was deciding what people
should watch without considering what people wanted to
watch. In effect, he was telling the pitchmen, who survived
by direct marketing, that they couldn't belong to the club;
that the club was for big businessmen who could afford to
play the TV game by the rules.

My agency heard the FCC's thunder and was rocked to
its very foundation. Virtually overnight my billings plum-
meted from $2.5 million to $400,000. Stations that had
accepted our commercials for years suddenly treated us like
lepers. Many refused any direct-marketing spots under any
conditions, fearful that the FCC would revoke their licenses.
Others accepted direct-response spots only if they were no
longer than two minutes. To tell a pitchman he had only 120
seconds to sell a product was like telling a conductor he had
two minutes to conduct a symphony.

For us, it was the bottom of the ninth, two outs, and
nobody on base. If we didn't find somebody or something
to come through in the clutch, the ball game was over.

But all entrepreneurs function best when their backs are
against the wall. We put all our chips on one idea; a long
shot, to be sure, but one that would pay off if it worked.

The idea had been simmering in the back of my mind
for a long time, and now was the time to try it. Basically, it
involved finding a chain of stores that would agree to exclusive distribution for direct-response items. At the end of the
commercial, we would merely substitute the names of the
stores for the phone number and address found in direct-
response spots. I dubbed this new concept Key Outlet Marketing (KOM).

At the time, many people thought Key Outlet Marketing
was a harebrained scheme, born out of desperation, and
doomed to failure. How, they asked, could anyone convince

a chain to take a lower profit margin and give mass display to a direct-response product? They looked at the entire program with a skeptical eye and wondered how one could make an effective two-minute retail commercial? And finally, the cynics sneered, "Can a Key Outlet commercial motivate enough people to go out of their way to a store and look for the product?"

The concept was unprecedented. And certainly it could result in monumental failure. But just as certainly, specific trends made the chains eager to be a part of Key Outlet Marketing. One of those trends was the sudden growth of discount houses. Discounters were lowballing the chains. Although the chains were getting 50 percent and 10 percent off a $1 retail price, they had to sell the product for 79 cents to compete with the discounters. With Key Outlet Marketing the chains could make 30 percent, a good reason to embrace the idea with open arms.

Second, in the early sixties, expressways began blossoming in every city, facilitating travel. These expressways made it easier for someone to leave his neighborhood and go to a chain store, even though it might be several miles away. Undoubtedly chains were to become the sine qua non for innovative retail products.

Finally, this was the era of the great shopping center explosion. Everywhere you looked, another mini-empire of stores was being built in the suburbs. And the chains made sure they were part of these shopping centers. People flocked to these shopping centers, often located near a newly built expressway, and business boomed.

All these things made Key Outlet distributed products easily available. The Key Outlet concept was like throwing a jigsaw puzzle against the ceiling and having all the pieces come down in place.

KOM was such a perfect concept, it was hard to believe it was legal. But of course it was. It circumvented the Robinson-Patman Act in that it did not discriminate against any one store. Rather, it worked in the same manner as a franchise operation.

No matter how perfect KOM seemed in theory, it had to be implemented. And so I began my search for a middle-man: someone with the "in" to deal effectively with the chains. What I was looking for was a first-class close-out man. A close-out man was a guy who bought up products for next to nothing, and resold then to the chains. This type of salesman and chain stores were blood brothers, and I needed the best close-out man to get my products into distribution. After much searching, I found Manny Gutter-man, "King of the Close-out Men." The chains worshiped him as if he were royalty. When he gave the chains a prod-uct, he gave them something that they could sell at a big profit.

As soon as I met Manny, I knew we could do business. He was a tough, hard-nosed salesman who "called 'em like he saw 'em" and had contacts on top of contacts. Manny was a legend in the business, and like all legends, it was tough to know which stories about him were true. What was true, however, was his clout.

Once, Manny had an appointment with a buyer from a major chain. The buyer kept Manny waiting for two hours. Finally, the buyer walked out of his office and said, "I can see you now." Manny gave him a withering glance and shouted, "Better take a good look because this is the last time you'll ever see me. I wouldn't sell you anything if you were the last buyer on earth, you son-of-a-bitch." Manny turned and strode out of the office.

Manny could get away with murder and often did. For instance, he once called Morrie Axelrod, the vice-president for merchandising at Thrifty Drugs in Los Angeles, and told him, "Send me an order for thirty-six thousand Handi-Screens at two dollars ten cents each."

Axelrod responded, "What are Handi-Screens?"

Manny screamed back, "What the hell do you care what they are—we're gonna spend twenty thousand dollars a week to sell them! Just send me the goddamned order." And Axelrod did just that, though he had no idea what he was buying.

Manny enjoyed such shows of strength. And when he

agreed to help me with my Key Outlet products, I was sure that I had found a general who would keep the troops in line.

Our first foray into Key Outlet Marketing was a hair cutter called the Hair Wiz. We had successfully sold it via direct response in the past. Manny approached the Sommers Drug Chain in San Antonio with a proposal. After explaining they would have exclusive distribution in the area, receive a 30 percent discount, and receive the benefit of a ten-second store tag at the end of the commercial, they were sold. After all, even if they didn't sell a product, the free advertising for their stores was worth a tag. Manny clinched the deal by offering them the same "money back, satisfaction guaranteed" that we offered consumers in our commercials. Calling it "return privilege," he explained that the chain could return any unsold merchandise for full credit.

They bought the concept because they knew that if customers, lured to the store by the commercials, didn't buy Hair Wiz, they could quite conceivably buy something else. With visions of crammed aisles and huge crowds, they gave us the go-ahead.

Of course, we were flying by the seat of our pants. At first, we had no idea how much time to buy. But we knew that there was a minimum expenditure that would assure us maximum TV discount rates. So we arbitrarily made that expenditure for three weeks of spots.

Our commercial incorporated as many benefits and as much demonstration as we could cram into 120 seconds. We bought inexpensive time based upon our sales resistance theory. The campaign for three weeks totaled $1,600 on three different San Antonio stations. We received about twenty-four spots a week for our money.

The Hair Wiz retailed for $2.98. With the 30 percent discount we gave Sommers, we received $2.10 for each unit sold. From $2.10, we subtracted the 35-cent cost of the unit, 12-cent administrative overhead, 21-cent sales cost, and 35 cents for projected net profit. The $1.07 we had left was what we could spend in advertising to sell one unit and make 35 cents. We called the $1.07 the "magic number.'' Based upon this magic number, we inventoried the market with 1.5 times the number of kits necessary to achieve our profit goals—this took into account that we were unlikely to sell every unit in every store. Thus we divided $1.07 into $1,600. We needed to sell approximately 1,500 units to reach our goal. Multiply that by 1.5 and we asked Sommers to put in 2,250 units. We also asked Sommers to supply us with an inventory each week so we could gauge the movement of the product. Thus, if we sold 1,500 Hair Wizes in three or four weeks, we could then restock the stores and start another three-week campaign. We could continue this strategy indefinitely as long as we were making a profit.

The Hair Wiz commercials aired, and we had to cancel all TV commercials after ten days. We didn't cancel because the Key Outlet approach was ineffective; we canceled because it was too effective! In just ten days, we had sold all the Hair Wizes in the market. It was then that I began to realize that Key Outlet Marketing wasn't just a survival technique for the Minow era. It was going to revolutionize marketing techniques.

Since the Hair Wiz campaign I have been working with Manny and his sons (Arthur and Steve, who have earned the respect of everyone in the business) for fifteen years and he has been greatly responsible for the sales success of such products as Tarn-X, Texative, Leak Sealer, TV Magic, Rapid Tape, Honey and Egg cream facial, Nu Vinyl, Nu-Finish, the Sun Shield, CLR Liquid Pour, and dozens of other products that gained national prominence and made the manufacturers wealthy.

As we grew, we also began to work with B & G Sales. Herman Goldenberg's organization reached out into the supermarket, hardware, and mail-order chain areas. Herman filled a need for the product that went beyond Key Outlet Marketing—handling products such as the Roll-O-Matic Mop, After Bite, Classic Nails, Dark Eyes, Long Nails, Chia Pet linen curlers. He added great strength to our marketing team.

8

Available at These Stores Only

Walgreens, Woolworth's, Eckert's, and every other chain in the country clamored to get in on the Key Outlet Marketing bonanza. Every Key Outlet product the Eicoff-Gutterman, Eicoff-Goldenberg combinations touched turned to gold. Like the sharpest tout at the track, we could pick a winner before the race began. We parlayed long shots into sure bets, and new clients with new products flocked to the agency.

Initially, all we were doing was finding a product that had enjoyed some success as a direct-response item and converting it to Key Outlet Marketing. There seemed to be no limit to the range of items. We were successful with housewares, chemicals, lawn and garden products, sewing appliances, and cosmetics. As an indication of how fast and furious a Key Outlet item could sell, there is the story of the Handi-Screen. It was a round screen with a handle used to cover a frying pan and keep the grease from splattering. For under $7,000, we created a commercial, bought time, and placed it in Key Outlets. Within a few months, the Handi-Screen had achieved distribution in over seventy markets.

Eventually, we sold more than 6 million units at $3.00 each.

Key Outlet Marketing infused direct-response products with new life. Direct-response advertising was and still is an inherently limited approach. Almost 50 percent of Americans won't buy products by mail no matter what is being sold. This 50 percent has a natural distrust of anything sold by mail. This distrust has been fostered, in part, by the few shysters in the business and the bad press direct marketing often receives. But this misguided opinion is also the result of people who ordered a direct-response product and never received it. These people naturally blame the advertiser, when in fact the fault lies with the post office, people who steal the package from the porch or foyer, or an honest error on the part of the seller or buyer.

Key Outlet Marketing brings all these distrustful people back into the marketplace. The positive effect of a well-known chain's association with a product cannot be underestimated. Suddenly, a product has been given a seal of credibility. The consumer reasons "If Walgreens is selling the thing, it has to be legitimate."

Key Outlet Marketing also has another great advantage: if you never saw the commercial, there is a chance the "point-of-sale display" could result in an "impulse" purchase.

Key Outlet has a seasonal advantage over direct response, which I call the Christmas bonus. In direct-response advertising, Christmas offers must be taken off the air around Thanksgiving because any orders received later than that would probably not get to the customer in time for Christmas. Obviously, many people don't buy Christmas gifts until a few weeks before the holiday. Key Outlet allows you to advertise until Christmas Day.

What makes Key Outlet Marketing work is the concept itself. It is a natural; it is not a synthetic strategy that has to be constantly adapted, refined, and reworked. It is plugging a round peg in a round hole: once you make the fit (put the product in the chains and the commercial on television), the Key Outlet concept gains momentum. For instance, it might seem that Key Outlet's fatal flaw is counter positioning in the chains. If the product is buried in a back aisle, it will die. But the "concept" prevents this from happening. First, you can't "hide" a Key Outlet product, no matter where it is. You must send each store a relatively large quantity of the product to make it work. Therefore, 200 or 300 units of any product will be an eye-catcher. Second, because the chain has exclusive distribution of the product, they will give it a prominent place in the store purely out of self-interest. And third, a Key Outlet product invariably dwarfs the competition. Remember that even big-name products stock only 10 or 20 units in each chain. Consequently, their display space appears puny next to a Key Outlet Marketing item.

Key Outlet Marketing evolved almost by itself. It was a natural evolution, and we discovered that it had inherent rules and regulations. We discovered that Key Outlet Marketing was unsuited to ma-and-pa stores and supermarkets. The ma-and-pa stores, especially in the seventies and eighties, just don't do enough "up-front" business to justify giving them a Key Outlet Marketing product. In the Chicago area, there are about 1,300 ma-and-pa drugstores, and 800 of them make most of their money from prescriptions.

Supermarkets, on the other hand, have the potential to be productive for Key Outlet. What prevents them from realizing that potential is their policy toward "in-out promotions." A classic example of that policy is when we sold 70,000 units of Handi-Screen in three weeks through a major food chain, but the chain refused to reorder, even though they were out of merchandise. They chose a literal interpretation of the "in-out promotion." The food chains are like country clubs: They might allow a Key Outlet product in as a guest, but they can't become a regular member. Their members are only those products that have passed through their screening committee, made it onto their computers, and then become "regular" items. Obviously, a Key Outlet product falls into another category, and the food stores have not yet found a way to keep that category available to their customers. The other chains—drug, variety, and hardware—

were and are perfectly willing to bend their rules to keep a fast-moving Key Outlet item in their stores.

The enormous effect Key Outlet Marketing can have on a product is graphically illustrated by the Dexter sewing machine. Its story demonstrates Key Outlet Marketing's power to revive a product that had received a premature burial. The marketplace is littered with the corpses of unique, beneficial products that should have been huge successes. The fact that they were not can be attributed to many factors: poor advertising, marketing, or distribution strategies. Still, anyone with a keen marketing eye can spot the ghosts of those products and bring them back to life with Key Outlet Marketing.

The Dexter sewing machine was born when Bernie Saltz, an inventor, hurled a challenge at me: "Give me an idea for a marketable product and I'll invent it." I accepted the challenge, and for the next few weeks racked my brain for the ultimate product; for a device that was flawless and peerless. Working at a fevered pitch, my mind spewed out concept after concept: zipperless pants, do-it-yourself fireplaces, four-wheeled bicycles. My dreams were awash with gears, levers, and blueprints as I tried to mesh them into a thing of purpose and beauty. And then it came to me. It was unique, beneficial, and would have mass appeal.

It was the ultimate sewing machine. It would be as portable and lightweight as a stapler, able to stitch and hem in places where other sewing machines dared not go. It should be able to sew drapes while they were hanging and hem a dress while it was being worn. With a triumphant gleam in my eye, I explained the idea to Saltz, who I knew had some experience with sewing machines in his soft-goods business.

Saltz began creating. One month later he unveiled the prototype: it resembled a pair of pliers with a needle. Somehow, I had envisioned a more grandiose embodiment of the idea. Still, the seed had been planted and we were going to watch it grow. Saltz redesigned the device a number of times until he designed something that looked more like a stapler. It had a tension knob, which adjusted the stitch size and tension, and a brilliantly conceived spring attachment held the thread for a pickup hook, virtually ensuring that the machine wouldn't miss a stitch. It was lightweight, attractive, and ready to go to market.

We named the invention the Dexter sewing machine, the "Dexter" connoting "hand" and "ambidextrous." Because the cost of producing the machine exceeded $70,000, I sought the aid of Lee Ratner's Grant Company, which agreed to finance the venture.

Our first live test was marginal, hovering in that purgatory between success and failure. Subsequent live tests were similarly marginal. Still, I had a hunch that if I could film the commercial and eliminate the mistakes that occurred on a live presentation, we'd have a winner on our hands. The Grant Company's executive committee wasn't so sure. They were against spending $70,000 for tools and dies. The project would have been scrapped then and there if it weren't for Ratner. He had confidence in my opinion. I had scored winners for him before, and he wasn't about to turn his back on me now. Facing his executive committee, he leveled them with a glance to let them know he meant business and said in his inimitable way, "If Al says he can sell the Dexter, he'll sell it. Let's make the product."

I made a commercial, aired it, and it worked. Thousands of orders began pouring in, and Ratner set up a production line. Then came an unexpected problem. The people who were quick to buy the Dexters were just as quick to return them. Although the handmade prototypes worked, there was a flaw when we went to mass production.

When I was called before Grant's executive committee, I walked into that room like a Mason facing the Spanish Inquisition: I had my faith, but they had the power. And they wielded that power mercilessly, "I told you so's" flying from their mouths like twenty lashes. Each of them raged against the folly of the project, the expense, the time wasted. Finally, I had had enough.

Turning to Ratner, I yelled, "I never said I could make the goddamned things. I only said I could sell them!"

At this point, Ratner put the whole argument in its

proper perspective: "Al's right, he never said he could make 'em, he only said he could sell 'em."

The production answer was a few months in coming, but when it came, it came in a big way. When you have a product like the Dexter sewing machine—a product that does something no other product has ever done before—it is essential that you convince the public that the thing actually works. No matter how good the commercial is, no matter how attractive the presentation, you need the credibility to clinch the deal. Key Outlet Marketing provided that credibility. When the public saw the Dexter sewing machine associated with Thrifty, Walgreens, Eckert's, and Woolworth's, they couldn't wait to start sewing drapes and hemming dresses. They couldn't wait to get their hands on a Dexter!

One indication that we had struck pay dirt came when Charlie Walgreen invited Manny Gutterman and me to his offices after the first Key Outlet campaign broke. When we sat down, he began, "I'd like to compliment you on the Dexter sewing machine campaign.

I responded, "I didn't think you'd know about it."

"When we sell a hundred thousand units of anything just in Chicago at five dollars each in seven weeks, I know," Mr. Walgreen responded.

Ultimately, the total sales of the Dexter sewing machine reached $25 million. And we wouldn't have sold one of them if Bernie Saltz hadn't challenged me to come up with an idea for the ultimate product; or if Lee Ratner wasn't stubborn enough to defy his executive committee and back me; and, what is most important, if I had never come up with a thing called Key Outlet Marketing. Because all those things came to pass, millions of drapes and skirts benefited, as did a few entrepreneurs.

As we began to channel more and more products into the Key Outlet formula, we honed our technique into a science. Our market budgets became scientific formulas, not based on "the seat of the pants" methods, and our method and selection of Key Outlets in each market became almost infallible.

Like any formula, however, Key Outlet Marketing is subject to misuse. Its volatile elements must be implemented correctly. If the formula is followed step-by-step, it often results in explosive sales. If it isn't, it occasionally blows up in an advertiser's face.

The danger is greatest when an advertiser has experienced excellent initial sales using Key Outlet Marketing. This advertiser rejects the gradual expansion that is the essence of Key Outlet Marketing. Instead, he attempts to add too many outlets too quickly to his distribution network to meet the demand for his product or service. Because Key Outlet Marketing is based on guaranteed sales—the advertiser agrees to take back any unsold inventory from his outlets— there is a great risk of tying up profits in inventories that are returned. Though the advertising-to-sales ratio might appear healthy, the reality is that a severe cash-flow problem often results if an advertiser overextends distribution.

As a result, he can't pay his advertising bills, and both his agency and the media stop his advertising, negatively affecting sales. On paper, his assets exceed his liabilities, but his attempt to become liquid fails because without advertising his inventory has virtually no value.

The way to prevent this from happening, of course, is to stick to the formula. Tight control must be maintained over the amount of merchandise inventoried and the number of outlets. The analogy to keep in mind is the one about the hungry man who orders more food than he can possibly eat: his eyes are bigger than his stomach. Similarly, do not let your appetite for success cause you to order more outlets than you can possibly use.

Another problem facing Key Outlet Marketing is its rejection of traditional approaches. The following case history illustrates what happens when Key Outlet Marketing and tradition clash swords.

When we finally decided to convert Donatelli Honey and Egg cream facial, a successful direct-response product, to retail, I prevailed upon Sanford Rose, president of Donatelli, to try Key Outlet Marketing. He had previously been highly successful introducing Imdrin, an arthritis and rheumatism product, through normal channels. When he finally gave the approval, Honey and Egg was an immediate success. Gray Drug in Cleveland, for instance, sold forty thousand jars in only six weeks, which constituted nearly 50 percent of their total cosmetic sales during this time. As his company grew, Rose decided to hire a marketing director: Ron Bliwas. He was a hotshot agency account executive who had worked on big name accounts at Ed Weiss & Associates. He took one look at our Key Outlet strategy and threw up his hands in despair. Though our advertising was indisputably effective, it was also—in Bliwas's eyes—indisputably bizarre. When he looked at our media-buying rates—which were far below that of Weiss's—he assumed that something was wrong—either we were creating phony affidavits or paying station reps under the table. Of course, that was not the case, but Bliwas didn't know what else to think. Also, he had never heard of an agency that discarded the traditional buying methods of "rating points," "reach," "cume," "cost per thousand," and "demographics" and instead relied on something called "the theory of sales resistance" and the "Isolation Factor" (the importance of a commercial running alone as opposed to within a commercial cluster). He was aghast at the length of our commercials. After all, everyone used thirty seconds as their base. Everyone knew the two-minute spot was an anachronism and, like the pitchman, should accept death gracefully.

The arguments we had over these points reached Olympian proportions. Bliwas would hurl thunderbolts and we would respond with lightning. He would thunder that a two-minute spot was less effective than a thirty-second spot. We would roar that a two-minute spot generated more sales than ten thirty-second spots. The argument raged back and forth, and, ultimately, we were forced to compromise. We agreed to change our buying patterns, attempting to factor in cost-per-thousand rating points when we made a buy. But how do you figure cost-per-thousand for a two-minute spot? We compromised by multiplying the audience by two to figure CPM, but the change caused sales to plummet and advertising costs to skyrocket.

Bliwas figured that the Honey and Egg sales had "leveled off"—that the incredible initial sales figures couldn't continue, and that they would have to be content with a lower level of sales. We knew this was not the case. In fact, we were positive that if we returned to our traditional buying methods, the Key Outlet strategy would tap a vast reservoir of customers that hadn't even been touched. After a number of heated discussions we were allowed to go back to our original strategy. Sales again soared!

There are two interesting footnotes to this story. First, the Honey and Egg facial literally became too hot to handle. We discovered that when it was shipped in the summer, the intense heat actually cooked the egg portion of the product, making it hard enough to bounce. No preservative was found to prevent this from happening, and this ended the successful reign of Honey and Egg as a top cosmetic product.

Second, Ron Bliwas came to work for the Eicoff agency (where he ultimately took over the presidency). If that seems strange (considering our heated exchanges over advertising methodology), it is also typical. In more than one case, we have converted "nonbelievers" like Bliwas to the Eicoff philosophy. It is simply a matter of first explaining to them how it works, and then showing them solid evidence that it does work. If they are like Bliwas—open-minded and aggressively intelligent—they fall in love with the beauty of the philosophy. And like any convert—a born-again Christian, for example—they embrace the philosophy more fervently than if they had practiced it all their lives. Bliwas became the best and smartest convert I had ever made.

9

A. Eicoff & Company's Greatest Hits

Using direct response to sell records wasn't a new idea. I had done it years ago on radio. But selling them on television was precedent-setting. To many advertising "pros," it seemed imbecilic. After all, television was a visual medium, and there was nothing demonstrable or visual about records. Yet our agency believed television would work for records. People buy records for many reasons besides the fact that they like the way they sound. They buy them because they set a mood; because they have sentimental value; because they are nostalgic; and because they confer status. And all these reasons to buy have a visual counterpart—romantic records conjure up the image of a young couple strolling hand in hand on the beach. If we could combine that visual image with the music, television would be a viable outlet for records.

Second, we felt that the collection of records we sold had to be unique. We could not sell the Beatles' latest album by direct marketing because anyone could buy it in a record store. What we needed was a record "not available in stores anywhere." The perfect record, I thought, would be one that would have all the earmarks of a collector's item.

Though the nostalgia craze had not yet swept the country, I recognized people's inherent longing for the "good old days" and the music of that era.

So, when Columbia House, a division of CBS, came to our agency with a record called "Best of the Big Bands," we decided to make a commercial that was literally smashing. Harry James was the announcer. He came on camera with a handful of old 78 RPM records, saying, "These records are collector's items," and then he dropped them on the floor. He stated, "Well, don't worry, now you can get them all on hi-fi 33⅓ RPM records." The point was made, the public bought it, and we soon had one record-breaking success after another.

Shortly thereafter we were responsible for the second-biggest-selling record offer in television. (The first was the Elvis Presley offer immediately after he died.)

Working with Columbia House, we came up with the idea for an album of classical music—the greatest hits from symphony and opera classics called "Music Masterpieces." Of course, the people in the Artist and Repertoire department at Columbia were completely negative about the idea . . . who's going to buy that stuff? they asked. Classical music buffs won't tarnish their phonograph needles with an unknown symphony playing snippets of the classics, they exclaimed. They will be insulted! And the kids who buy records, they wailed, they won't buy it in a million years.

After much pleading, Bob Berg, my creative director and senior VP, and I convinced them to give it a try. The commercial featured a very distinguished, erudite English gentleman, John Williams, standing in front of a harp in an elegant, wood-paneled room. In the most refined of tones, he asked whether anyone knew that popular movie themes and songs were derived from the classics; that "Full Moon and Empty Arms" was originally composed by Rachmaninov; that the themes from "Elvira Madigan" and "2001" were based in classical music. What we were selling was instant culture, and like instant coffee, it was easy to make and looked like the real thing.

Never had an offer been so successful on television. We

sold millions of records—everybody from teenagers to oc-
togenarians bought them. Why? Because we had taken classical music down from the exclusive pedestal on which it
was usually placed and made it accessible to the masses.
People who would never buy Beethoven's Fifth were suddenly buying the album because they could actually hum
some of the tunes! Teenagers, weaned on loud guitars and
raucous drums, found that there was a certain status at-
tached to owning a classical album. They could say to their
parents and girl friends, "Look, I've got Culture." Perhaps
they never played it, but I'd bet anything they displayed it
prominently for people to see. Even classical music buffs
bought it, perhaps to give their children a taste of the great
composers. It was the only record offer we ever had that
covered the entire spectrum of record buyers.

A. Eicoff & Company soon became the hottest artist on
the charts, a group that guaranteed gold records for all. We
sold virtually every type of record imaginable: "Italian Love
Songs," "Fabulous Fifties," Glenn Miller, Johnny Mathis,
"Top of the Hit Parade," Mills Brothers, Ink Spots, Brook
Benton, Sesame Street, Disney, Ray Charles, and on and on.

About this time, we also developed a subgenre of direct-response advertising, a format to sell subscriptions for
newspapers and magazines. Until we developed this format,
most publications avoided trying to sell subscriptions on TV,
relying on direct mail and inserts in their publications. Their
television advertising was image-oriented, designed to sub-
tly sell people on the "idea" of their magazine or newspaper, hoping these spots would increase newsstand sales.
But in the seventies, when postal rates and printing costs
skyrocketed, many of these publications no longer had a use
for subtle, image-oriented advertising. They needed a
method that would show demonstrable results—that would
rope in subscribers fast and furiously. And that is where we
entered the picture. We explained to publications our cost-
effective advertising/marketing methods—how we could
test their magazine on television for under ten thousand dollars and how if the subscriptions gained didn't pay for the

advertising cost, they could walk away with a minimum capital expenditure.

For subscription-hungry magazines, it was an offer they couldn't refuse. We began creating and testing commercials for a wide variety of publications—Time, Newsweek, Sports Illustrated, Mother Earth News, Sports Afield, the Detroit Free Press, Bass Anglers, and Playboy.

Time-Life Books suggested we approach the circulation department of Sports Illustrated magazine to see if they would run a test. Because of the minimal budget, they agreed. Our program was an instant success; not only did we bring in subscriptions at less than 50 percent of the projected desirable cost, but we did so even in markets where Sports Illustrated magazine never was successful (because those markets lacked major league sports teams).

Sports Illustrated magazine was not an anomaly. We increased subscriptions for virtually every publication we handled. And we did it using our formula: a demonstration of how reading that particular magazine would be beneficial to the consumer. Using pictures from the magazine, the commercials featured an announcer who would tantalize the viewer with descriptions of the pleasures he was missing. If it was a newsmagazine, we would stress the information-benefit of the publication. If it was a feature-oriented magazine, we would emphasize the entertainment-benefit. In rapid succession, story after story would be bannered by the words and pictures of the commercial, building in intensity so that the viewer became convinced that the publication was "essential" reading. By the end of the spot, the viewer looked at the publication the way he looked at some marvelous new kitchen appliance—it was something he had to have.

During the seventies, we developed another enormously effective tool for savvy advertisers to use. Support Advertising was born when Columbia House came to us with a problem: they wanted to advertise their record club on television. It was a tough problem. By definition, record-club offers require the listing and choice of numerous record selections. How could one choose thirteen albums for one dollar from a TV commercial? It was virtually impossible. It seemed that print was the only viable medium for such offers.

But television was an effective medium for selling records. Perhaps we could shape it to fit the product. Our idea began with this premise: record clubs, book clubs, insurance policies all need signed commitments, which you can't get directly on TV. Yet because of a magazine or newspaper's relatively limited audience, many people never take advantage of these offers simply because they are not aware of them. A television commercial that is frequently repeated often reaches a numerically greater audience than a print ad and can open an entirely new market for these offers. If the commercial is motivating, it can send people out in droves looking for offers in their local newspapers, in magazines, or even in their mailboxes.

In theory, it sounded workable. Of course, advertisers would necessarily be reluctant to buy that theory. They would be paying for television time that would not result in measurable sales. TV would simply be priming the pump.

Still, Columbia House was interested, and we made our first support commercial. Amazingly, their record club memberships increased rapidly. News of the success spread through the business, and we soon were besieged with similar requests for that odd, new advertising strategy called "support."

Of course, it was "seat-of-the-pants" time again. How much should you spend on support?—50 percent of the primary medium buy? 70 percent? 80 percent? 100 percent? 250 percent? We tried them all. When should the support run—Thursday? Friday? Saturday? or Friday, Saturday, Sunday? Support was so effective that almost everything worked. But everything worked precisely because we were lucky and not because we knew what we were doing.

After extensive post-analysis research, we zeroed in on the most effective expenditures on a market-by-market basis. We found that any ratio of the cost of the support media to the primary media was completely erratic. You must spend three times as much to support a six-page insert as a two-page insert, using a percentage of primary-to-secondary media ratios. This is ridiculous because logic tells you you should spend more to call attention to the less obvious ad.

We found the crucial factor in support advertising's success was that the primary medium must achieve at least 35 percent penetration in the secondary medium's Area of Dominant Influence (ADI). In other words, if the newspaper doesn't reach a significant percentage of the television or radio audience (the support media), then the support commercial is reaching too many people who can't obtain the print ad.

For instance, in Chicago, neither the Tribune newspaper nor the Sun Times has 35 percent market penetration. You would have to use both to achieve enough minimal penetration for TV support to work. Most agencies who have ventured into support advertising have failed to recognize this. When they run a support program—and it fails—they often wrongly blame the concept. Support advertising, when used properly, is the most effective direct-marketing concept we have ever used. We have achieved results beyond our most optimistic projections. We have made workday ROP (runs of paper) ads work. We have made periodicals work that never worked before without support.

Achieving 35 percent market penetration in the primary medium requires a certain creativity, but it is easily attainable. Depending on the market, there are a variety of combinations that will produce that 35 percent figure. In Seattle, for instance, you cannot simply buy the Seattle newspaper and hope to reach 35 percent of the ADI, but if you add the Tacoma paper you have achieved the penetration objective. In some markets, you can supplement a newspaper with direct mail. In others, you can combine one print buy with TV Guide magazine or other periodicals.

When support is coordinated properly, it results in an immediate, demonstrable increase in sales (or membership).

That increase is often so dramatic that the advertiser is un-
sure how to react.

A few years ago, Scott Paper Company came to us and
asked if we could produce a support campaign for a premium, clothlike paper towel they were introducing called Job
Squad. We created a support commercial and tested it in
two markets: Peoria, Illinois, and Davenport, Iowa. The support programs' sole purpose was to increase newspaper
coupon redemption.

After the campaign broke, we discovered what seemed
to be a fatal error: the Iowa newspapers inadvertently
printed the same ad run in the Illinois papers with the stipulation: "Valid Only for Residents of Illinois." That meant
there could be no redemption of these coupons in Iowa.
Normally, a good coupon redemption averages 2 percent to
3 percent of a paper's circulation. The Davenport paper's
circulation was around 200,000, meaning that without support, the ad could generate between 4,000 to 6,000 redemptions. Considering the "Not Valid" statement, we felt
we would be lucky if we came anywhere close to those
figures.

Our support, however, generated 50,000 redemptions
in both Illinois and Iowa, which was 700 percent over the
normal redemption rate! Why? Well, for one thing, the people in Iowa seemed to ignore the "Not Valid" statement.
But, more important, the enormous selling power of the
support rendered the normal coupon redemption rate ob-
solete. It caused those newspaper ads for Job Squad to
stand out like boldface headlines on page one. Most coupon offers rely on a consumer noticing the offers while leaf-
ing through the paper. That reliance stacks the deck against
a good redemption rate. But support calls attention to the
coupon ad, giving the economy-minded consumer an incentive to look and clip the ad.

If support is so effective, why is it not embraced univer-
sally by advertisers? For the same reason many of the advertising techniques detailed in this book are ignored: They
don't conform to standard perceptions of how things are

done. For instance, when Scott discovered the incredible response their ads were getting, they were horrified. "You boosted the redemption rate so high, you're wrecking our budgets," they explained. "All these redemptions will throw our advertising budget out of line."

"But why offer coupon redemptions if you don't want the coupons redeemed," I asked. I received blank looks for an answer. Obviously, support advertising requires more vision than most middle-management bureaucrats possess.

10

Cigarette Smoking Is Hazardous to Television's Health

In 1969, the television industry received the bad news: cigarette advertising would be banned forever. That meant an estimated loss of $270 million in yearly revenues at a time when many stations were just beginning to realize a profit. Throughout the country, television stations pressed the panic button: either they found a new source of revenue or they would have serious problems.

The Television Bureau of Advertising (TVB), an organization of television stations, desperately began to search for new sources of revenue. After extensive research, they decided that their best bet was direct-response advertising. Their study revealed that major companies like Columbia House, Time-Life, Newsweek, and Reader's Digest were spending millions of dollars in direct mail. If those companies could be induced to spend some of that money on television direct response, the new revenue would help replace the lost income from cigarette advertising.

In 1969, there were virtually no direct-response spots from major companies on the air. The exception was CBS's Columbia House, an account of our agency. So it came as no surprise when Jake Evans, one of the top TVB executives, came knocking on my door asking how they could get big direct-response advertisers to use television.

It was ironic. When Newton Minow had come to power in the early sixties, direct response was viewed as the black sheep in the television family and was nearly exiled from the airwaves. Now, it was being courted as television's salvation.

I did not mince words when I explained to Jake exactly what must be done if they wanted to bring direct-response advertisers into the fold. First, I told him they would have to change their attitude toward direct response. No longer could they look at the direct marketer as a two-dollar whore. In the past, direct-response advertising was accepted only as a last resort. The attitude was: "If you haven't gotten laid yet, you might as well grab whatever's available, no matter how sleazy." I told them that not only was that attitude insulting to direct marketers, but it totally disregarded direct marketing's potential. All other media, including Cosmopolitan magazine, TV Guide, Playboy, Time, Newsweek, the New York Times, regarded direct marketing as a sophisticated marketing strategy capable of eliciting an incredible response.

I also explained that TV stations would have to overcome their prejudice against the 90- and 120-second spots. "Trying to fit a direct-response spot in a thirty-second slot," I told them, "is like putting a fat lady into a miniskirt."

Finally, I delivered the coup de grâce. I explained that stations would have to adjust their rate structures: direct marketers could not and would not pay the same rates as everyone else.

But I also added that a separate rate structure was justified. Most newspapers and magazines had employed a separate rate structure for direct marketers for years. The rationale was that direct marketers are a different breed of advertising animal. Unlike most advertisers, they don't have a preconceived idea of what their schedule will be. Their budget is flexible and solely dependent on how the media pulls. If a station can pull orders for a direct marketer, it is conceivable that he ultimately might spend as much as $100,000 a week on that station. The point is that the direct marketer's budget is based on instant results. He starts small and builds, depending on the orders he receives. So it is to a station's advantage to give the direct marketer a preferred rate so he is sure to pay out.

TVB studied the information I gave them and incorporated it into two presentations—one for the television stations and the other for major direct marketers. Both groups responded to the presentation positively. Direct-marketing companies began flooding TVB's switchboard with calls, and TVB referred them to A. Eicoff & Company. Television stations let us write their rate cards if we would throw some business their way. It was a fecund environment, which helped the agency grow enormously.

We were sought by major corporations that, prior to TVB's efforts, never gave our agency a second glance. Time-Life, Amoco, Fingerhut, Playboy, Mattel, Reader's Digest, Longines Symphonette, Warner Brothers Records, Capitol Records, Hansen Publishing, Avon Inc., Meredith Publishing Inc., were among the companies that soon became clients.

The idea of reaching a mass audience with a minumum financial risk was enticing. Eliminating the limitations imposed by the print medium—relatively small audiences, the inability to demonstrate the product—was a strong argument in television's favor. The fact that TV' commercials could be placed or pulled almost instantly compared to the four-to-six-week deadlines of magazines opened new vistas. The direct marketer had been presented with millions of new prospects, gift-wrapped and ready for delivery.

Suddenly, our direct marketing skills were in great demand. Combined with Key Outlet, we had a formidable one-two punch. In the next few years, television direct-marketing revenues exploded across the board. From 1970 to 1973, TV revenues from direct marketers increased from around $12 million to $100 million. For helping in this area, TVB presented me with their Pioneering Award. I am one of the

A young Alvin Eicoff, displaying d-Con, one of the great success stories in radio advertising history

The Entrepreneurship & Business Development Class
of the

Graduate School of Business Administration
University of California, Berkeley

hereby recognizes

Alvin M. Eicoff

as

BUSINESS FACULTY LECTURER
"summa cum laude"

presented by the undersigned
with thanks
for many years of distinguished service as a member of our guest faculty

Earl F. Cheit, Dean   Leo B. Hazel   Richard H. Holton

These products represent over $500 million in sales volume. All of them were (and many still are) Eicoff accounts and were sold via direct response or Key Outlet Marketing. Among the more familiar names are Time-Life Books, Nu-Vinyl, Tarn-X, and TV Magic. (1978)

Bob Berg, creative director/senior vice-president, A. Eicoff & Company, presents an award to Arthur Heydendael of Time-Life Books in honor of the making of the agency's 2,000th commercial.

Jacob Evans of the Television Bureau of Advertising presents the prestigious TVB Award to Alvin Eicoff "in gratitude and recognition of his pioneering and development of successful television direct response." The only other Chicagoan to receive this award was Lenny Lavin of Alberto Culver. (1972)

Product: Tarn-X   Client: Jelmar   Year: 1966
The success of this product demonstrates how you can take a relatively old product in an old package and revitalize it, using a unique demonstration. We created commercials that showed in graphic detail how Tarn-X removed tarnish. This retail product soon became the leader in its product category and has retained its position to this day.

Product: Nu-Vinyl   Client: Reed Union   Year: 1973
Our client came to our agency with an idea for a new product: one that would protect the vinyl tops of cars through rain and shine and maintain a high gloss. We tested this product with a highly unusual demonstration commercial. In the commercial, we treated one-half of a car's vinyl top with Nu-Vinyl, then ran it through a car wash fifty consecutive times. The effectiveness of Nu-Vinyl was established, and soon the product established itself as the biggest seller in its field.

Product: Nu-Finish   Client: Reed Union   Year: 1975
Our client wanted us to introduce a car polish via TV commercials. The problem was that big companies such as Turtle Wax, S. C. Johnson, and DuPont had a stranglehold on the market. We broke that stranglehold with a commercial for Nu-Finish, the first poly-based car polish on the market. Using a unique demonstration—applying Nu-Finish to a car in a junkyard— we achieved 40–50 percent of the auto-wax market within our limited area of distribution and ultimately became a leading brand in the field.

Product: Liberace Song Book   Client: Hansen House   Year: 1974

"How-to" books are perfect products for direct-response advertising, and Liberace's book on how to learn to play the piano was the most perfect of them all. We created a demonstration commercial using Liberace as the spokesperson, and we sold 500,000 books in three years. The book is still selling!

Product: Playboy Magazine   Client: Playboy   Year: 1976

Our work for Playboy was and is precedent-setting advertising. First, we continually have increased their subscription and newsstand sales via direct-response commercials, thereby erasing all doubts as to direct-response TV's effectiveness in selling a print publication. Second, we created tasteful, image-conscious spots for a men's magazine that were also motivational. Our work for Playboy has helped establish A. Eicoff & Company's reputation as the leader in the field of direct-response advertising for print publications.

Product: Vita Mix   Client: Vita Mix   Year: Early 1950s
The spokesperson in this early pitchman commercial is also the product's manufacturer. His name is Bill Barnard, and he helped make Vita Mix a household word. In this incredible thirty-minute commercial, Barnard pulled out all the stops to create the ultimate demonstration commercial.

Alvin Eicoff demonstrates his affection for books that have a unique perspective on the business world. One of Mr. Eicoff's favorite books is called "How to Make a Million Dollars in the Mail Order Business." It is one of his favorites because the man who wrote the book made one million dollars selling his book by mail order!

Client: Grant Company   Product: Salad Maker   Year: 1950
The Salad Maker commercial ran for 8 minutes 27 seconds! It included a tag that ran 1 minute 33 seconds (the length of the tag was the result of needing seven separate phone numbers for the New York City area). In the first two years the commercial aired, over 4 million Salad Makers were sold at $2.98. Four million more were sold in the next three years at $3.98.

Client: Winston Sales   Product: Fishing Kit   Year: 1960
Bill Stern, famous sports announcer, and Red Fisher, member of the Fishing Hall of Fame, teamed up to sell the 296-piece Winston Fishing Kit for $8.95. Over 1,200,000 units were sold before the Newton Minow "wasteland" speech forced the Fishing Kit to be the first Key Outlet Marketing experiment. Using Sommers Drug Chain in San Antonio, Texas, as the first Key Outlet, our commercial helped sell another 800,000 units at $9.95. A new commercial featuring Red Fisher and Frank Gifford was equally successful.

Client: Columbia House   Product: Music Masterpiece   Year: 1971
Despite the initial negative reaction of Columbia House's Artist and Repertoire Department, this record became the second all-time best-seller
among albums offered on television via direct response. (First was the Elvis
Presley album aired the day after he died.) We reached the entire projected
dollar volume and profit quota for Columbia in these months of exposure.
In twenty-four months, 1,800,000 albums were sold; the commercial
made in 1971 was still running in 1981.

Product: Sona   Client: Grant Company   Year: 1954
This was a skin-toned lipstick used to retouch dark circles under eyes and
eliminate lines and wrinkles. Initially, the television introduction of this
product was handled by Les Persky & Company, which generated sales of
375,000 units at $2.98 in ninety days. Unfortunately, no one was exerting
any control over this runaway success. At about this point, I went in and
helped make this control a reality.

Product: Handi-Screen   Client: BBI   Year: 1963

Handi-Screen was a wire-mesh device that kept grease from flying out of a frying pan or wok. This product is the perfect example of pricing a product according to what it does rather than what it costs to manufacture. If we used the latter criterion as a basis for pricing, Handi-Screen would sell for only 89 cents. But because the Handi-Screen was such a valuable product for the housewife, preventing grease from burning her hands or making her kitchen a mess, we priced it at $2.98. Ultimately, we sold 4 million Handi-Screens in two years. As a footnote, I might say that the need for this product still exists. Yet most housewives are not even aware of the product's existence due to a lack of advertising. An advertising campaign—if executed properly—could move 4 million units again.

Product: Brook Benton   Client: Longines Symphonette   Year: 1975

The success of this album proves that you don't have to be a superstar to sell records via direct-response television advertising. This album sold for $6.95 and became one of the all-time best-sellers—in excess of 400,000 units in less than six months on the air. Longines had a number of top-selling, direct-response-advertising albums, including the Mills Brothers, Ink Spots, and Ray Charles.

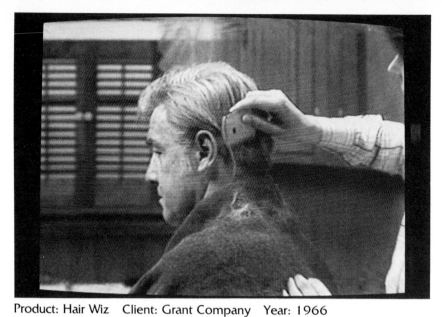

Product: Hair Wiz   Client: Grant Company   Year: 1966
When the price of a haircut jumped from $1 to $3 virtually overnight, the market was ready for a do-it-yourself hair-cutter—the Hair Wiz. It was another excellent example of pricing a product according to what it can do rather than what it costs to manufacture. For instance, with a three-and-a-half-times markup, Hair Wiz could have been sold at $1 and still turned a profit. But we knew that people would be more than willing to pay $3, because a customer had only to use the product once and it paid for itself.

In addition, the commercial graphically demonstrated how easy the Hair Wiz worked, beginning with the line, "If you can read numbers, you can cut hair." This ease-of-use, combined with its money-saving potential, proved irresistible: 7 million units at $2.98 and still selling well.

Product: Time-Life Books   Client: Time Inc.   Year: 1972
Over the past eleven years, we have worked with Time Inc. to produce

some of the most effective direct-response advertising in the history of television. We have sold thousands upon thousands of sets of Time-Life books, turning the art of selling books on television into an exact science. Whether the subject of the book is the Old West or World War II, we have consistently produced motivational, profitable advertising.

Product: TV Magic   Client: M. B. Magic   Year: 1972
Armed only with a deck of magic cards and a $7,000 advertising budget, Rick Carey and Marshall Brodein came to our agency and asked what we could do for them. What we did was create direct response and Key Outlet commercials for TV Magic, resulting in $300,000 net profit in the first year, $700,000 in the second year, and over $1 million in the third year.

Rick Carey soon became the sole owner of the largest manufacturers of retail magic products in the country. Unfortunately, he tried to become too big, too quickly, and overextended himself. Though TV Magic remained profitable, the profits were tied up in inventory, and he couldn't pay bills with inventory. Overexpansion is a common mistake among aggressive, relatively inexperienced advertisers. That is why I generally recommend that companies gradually expand their advertising on a market-by-market basis.

Though TV Magic failed because of this overexpansion, it was reborn when it was bought by Marshall Brodein, and he recently made $400,000 on a $100,000 investment.

Photoboards for Famous Television Commercials

PLAYBOY MAGAZINE
SUBSCRIPTION OFFER

(MUSIC)
PLAYBOY -- the one magazine that brings it all together for you each month.

Playboy reflects your appreciation of the total good life. It reflects your good taste in fashion...fun... fiction...and fact.

You get first-rate reviews of books, movies and television shows.

Playboy puts you where the action is...in sports...in music...and on the set.

Playboy's Advisor column lets you share the personal experiences and candid opinions of others.

While Playboy's life style pages are packed with insights and tips on how to get the most out of your life.

Each month the PLAYBOY Interview uncovers the real person behind the personality.

And Playboy's pictorials are often news-makers in themselves. Every month Playboy discovers and presents the world's most beautiful women.

For the man who wants it all, Playboy brings it all together--issue after issue. As a subscriber you're sure to enjoy Playboy each and every month.

And right now, you can get 12 big, beautiful issues delivered to you at half the newsstand price.

Subscribe to Playboy and start enjoying life to its fullest.

To order your subscription, here's all you do:

Playboy

DOMAN INDUSTRIES
TARN-X

Remember when cleaning your silver meant hours of hard work, rubbing and scrubbing until your hands were raw?

Well, ladies, those days are gone forever. Now there's an amazing product...called Tarn-X ...

that foams away tarnish from sterling, silver-plate, copper and gold, even platinum and diamonds.

Watch how easy it is to clean this badly tarnished spoon. Just dip...no rubbing... no buffing...isn't that amazing?

To clean deep crevices and intricate patterns, just wipe on Tarn-X...even deeply embedded tarnish rinses away like magic.

Did you ever see a copper cleaner that works this easy? Tarn-X will save you hours in the kitchen.

This bottle contains more Tarn-X than you'll probably use at home in a year, yet it costs only $3.00.

And it's guaranteed to work for you at home as quickly and easily as it does here on TV...or return it to place of purchase for your money back.

Doman Industries, Tarn-X

MATTEL GROUP
KNITTING MACHINE

Imagine...being able to make gorgeous knitted items like this beautiful afghan...

or this magnificent pillow -- and WITHOUT knowing how to knit!

Well, if you can turn a crank and sew on a button, you can make any of these items and more -- with this amazing automatic home knitting machine.

Here's how it works. Just thread the machine. This tension bar automatically keeps the stitches perfectly uniform.

Now just turn the handle. That's all there is to it! A few turns and you've made a small tube.

Close the ends of the tube and you have a Granny Circle.

Rows of Granny Circles make this winter scarf...

Continue to turn and make a long tube, to create these adorable stuffed animals.

Yes, there's just no limit to the things you can create -- sweaters, hats, pillows bedspreads, purses, infant wear...and what a time-saver!

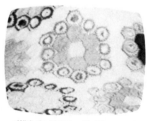

With the Knitting Machine, you can actually make this magnificent afghan in a fraction of the time it would take to knit by hand.

The Knitting Machine comes complete with a skein of yarn, plus step-by-step instructions and patterns to make all the things you see here...

$14.95

and, the price is only $14.95! Best yet, the Knitting Machine carries a full one year warranty. If dissatisfied, return it for replacement or a full refund

Phoenix Group, a division of Mattel

REED UNION CORP.
NU VINYL

If your car's vinyl top looks old, weather beaten, dull...

now you can restore its original show room beauty with NU VINYL, the fantastic vinyl and leather care product.

Just wipe NU VINYL on. There's no rubbing, no buffing and just one application will protect your vinyl top month after month.

We ran this car through 50 consecutive car washes, yet in spite of all the scrubbing, the harsh detergents and steam, the side treated with NU VINYL still shines like new.

It's great for your car's vinyl upholstery, too.

NU VINYL is perfect for all of your vinyl and leather goods. Protects expensive vinyl and leather covered furniture from stains and scratches.

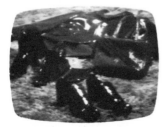

Restores the shine to scuffed-up shoes, boots and purses.

So restore the original beauty and luster and protect all your vinyl and leather goods with NU VINYL. It's guaranteed to perform to your complete satisfaction or return it for a full refund.

Reed Union Corp, Nu-Vinyl

ROLL-O-MATIC® MOP & WAXER
M. B. WALTON, INC.

1. Ladies, take another look... a good look... at the completely new and different sponge head you'll find now...

2. on the famous ROLL-O-MATIC, the original, self-wringing mop and waxer.

3. It's the all new T35S Kleen-Rite™ sponge head...a product of space-age research and development made exclusively for ROLL-O-MATIC.

4. The new T35S is far more durable... it won't shred, tear or get hard.

5. And it's resistant to bacteria build-up, so the ROLL-O-MATIC will never have that sour, old mop odor.

6. It's also 25% more absorbent. Just look how easily the ROLL-O-MATIC glides across the floor soaking up water.

7. For wringing and rinsing... simply flip the lever... it's that easy.

8. The improved roller action covers the entire head to squeeze out every drop of water.

9. There's no more bending, stooping or straining-- and your hands never touch the dirty water.

10. And because the ROLL-O-MATIC won't drip... you'll find it one of the easiest ways to wash walls-- and hard to reach ceilings.

11. You'll find the ROLL-O-MATIC is also ideal for spreading liquid wax... thinly and evenly, without streaking.

12. But best of all, the T35S Kleen-Rite sponge head always stays soft and absorbent...

13. so even the messiest spills, like chocolate syrup, can be whisked away quickly and easily.

14. Yes, we're constantly working to make the ROLL-O-MATIC better than ever... to make your work easier than ever.

15. So get the ROLL-O-MATIC today. Satisfaction guaranteed or return it to place of purchase for a full refund.

16. New T35S Kleen-Rite refill heads will fit the original ROLL-O-MATIC.

M. B. Walton, Roll-O-Matic

few Chicagoans ever to receive this coveted award. Despite my dislike of awards, I was proud to receive this one. It meant acceptance by a segment of the industry that has never before accepted the precedent-setting strategies of this maverick advertising man.

Even with this award and TVB's endorsement, we were still not part of the status quo. In the early seventies, when we started talking seriously with Fortune 500 companies about their advertising, many viewed us warily. After all, we did not waltz into their boardrooms with fifty storyboards. We had no dog and pony shows, our account executives did not hang from chandeliers, and there were no audiovisual pyrotechnics. Instead, we merely explained the Eicoff method of advertising and marketing. Many of the executives we talked to were intrigued by it, but their doubts were aroused as soon as we mentioned the budget. When we asked for only $10,000 (or less) to prove the validity of our concept, they balked.

I will never forget when we first approached Time-Life Books. They had just finished running a thirty-second direct-marketing spot for their book series and the campaign had failed miserably. Their agency had spent over $125,000, and the commercial hadn't worked. When I mentioned to Arthur Heydendahl of Time-Life that I could make a successful direct-response commercial and test at $10,000, he shook his head in dismay. "Even if you could," he said, "after our hundred-twenty-five-thousand-dollar fiasco, it would make us look pretty bad. Come back in six months when the memory of that failure isn't fresh in their minds."

Six months later I returned and talked with John Conova. When I mentioned the low budget, he stated, "I can get fifty thousand dollars easier than I can get ten thousand dollars." Then his eyes lit up. "Tell me you need fifty thousand dollars, so I can present it to the committee."

"But I don't need that much," I protested.

"Don't worry about it."

I started worrying only when Time-Life decided to give us a chance. They gave us a series of books called The Emergence of Man, which they had sold through print ads. It had virtually stopped selling, and they wanted to know if direct-response TV could do anything for the book. Using only $7,000 of the allocated $50,000 I decided to revive Lazarus. If Emergence of Man worked, I knew that Time-Life would evolve into one of our biggest clients.

We crafted a two-minute commercial whose very first frames couldn't help but whet the viewer's curiosity. Opening with a striking shot of something that was half-man, half-ape, the announcer stated, "Two million years ago, this man roamed the earth . . ." As the spot unfolded, we gradually built up the mystery of man's origins, using the beautiful pictures in the Time-Life book. We developed a pulsating rhythm that hooked viewers, using quick cuts, zooms, and pans of caves, ancient tools, and fossils as the announcer's awestruck voice narrated man's evolution. When we made the offer of the Time-Life book, explaining that it was a ten-day free trial offer, the viewer couldn't help but reach for the phone. The offer evolved naturally from the presented material, seamlessly woven into the substance of the commercial. Of course, our skill in buying time in highly motivating periods helped the commercial achieve its objective.

Emergence of Man subsequently sold thousands of copies, and Time-Life became a steady and satisfied client. Virtually every series we advertised became a profit-maker. No matter what the topic was—gardening, a history of World War II, the Old West, home repair—we treated it like a product. In other words, the commercials actually "demonstrate" the books. They are like trailers for a feature film, highlighting the most intriguing scenes and causing the viewer to want to know the complete story. Knowledge is the product we're selling, and we illustrate how that knowledge can be beneficial to the viewer. For instance, understanding the mystery of evolution carries a cultural benefit—everyone understands the appeal of discovering one's roots.

11

How to Create Commercials That Create Sales

Many creative people find it difficult to make effective, motivating commercials. They can make slice-of-life spots, create aesthetically pleasing animated spots, and dream up comic vignettes that tickle your funnybone. But a realistic, demonstration-type commercial—one that focuses on the true benefits of a product—is the one that's most difficult to write. The creative departments of many agencies aren't trained to make straightforward, realistic commercials that tell the product story in the simplest possible way.

We're back to the pitchman technique. In earlier chapters I have shown how pitchmen created the perfect sales pitch and, eventually, the perfect commercial. In my opinion, the best commercials evolve directly from this technique. The essence of the approach is to set forth the problem, explain the solution, and then demonstrate why a specific product best meets that solution.

Sound simple? In theory, perhaps. But putting the theory into practice is another matter entirely. There is the saying: The shortest distance between two points is a straight line. Similarly, the shortest distance between seller and buyer is a straightforward presentation. Unfortunately, some copywriters take unnecessary detours on their way to making a sale. They take detours because they want aesthetically pleasing award winners. What often results is an irrational approach to a rational product. Do the ferocious animals in car commercials really motivate anyone to buy cars? Are cute, animated cartoon characters better salesmen than real, live people? Absolutely not!

But too many copywriters don't understand this. They don't understand that when they write a commercial they are knocking on someone's door and asking to come into their living room. If they would use this frame of reference, they wouldn't come into the living room with animated beavers, chorus lines, or semipornographic models. As invited guests, they don't have that privilege. They are there not to entertain but to sell.

The first step in selling is to state the problem—then tell how the product solves the problem. If this seems obvious, then why do the majority of commercials fail to do this? Too often, they opt for some attention-getting device that is at best tangentially related to their product.

Too often, the opening shot of a commercial is wasted setting the audience up for a joke or creating "atmosphere." These openings, upon repeated viewings, lose their humor or are merely distracting.

In most instances, the first visual and audio elements of a commercial should state the problem clearly and concisely. The potential customer should feel a strong personal identification with the problem presented, reflexively nodding his head in acknowledgment. The opening audio should reinforce the visual presentation in an attention-getting, authentic, and credible manner.

An excellent example of this technique is the Roll-O-Matic mop commercial. The opening shot is of a housewife laboring to mop a kitchen floor. The audio begins: "One of the most tiring, backbreaking household chores is scrubbing and waxing floors . . . the constant bending, stooping, and straining to wring out your mop."

A commercial cannot set up a problem faster, more effectively, than that. The words have an almost visceral kick to them. When the announcer says "bending, stooping, and straining," any woman watching the commercial immediately reacts. Those words are a trigger; once they're uttered, the viewer immediately thinks, "That's me." Stringing together adjectives with negative connotations builds the intensity of a problem so that the viewer is subconsciously compelled to seek relief, to find an outlet for that intensity. By demonstrating the benefits of the Roll-O-Matic mop, the commercial provides that outlet.

Choosing the manner in which a product is demonstrated is crucial. Because most products can be demonstrated in a variety of ways, the creative team must pinpoint the one demonstration with the most universal appeal. The more problems the demonstration solves, the greater the chances of motivating the viewer to buy the product.

Following this strategy, the Nu-Finish car polish commercial demonstrates the product in a junkyard and shows how Nu-Finish puts a lustrous sheen on the oldest, most battered car's surface. The demonstration had a double-barreled impact. For owners of old cars, Nu-Finish demonstrates its efficacy beyond a shadow of a doubt. New car owners watching the demonstration are led to believe, "If it works so well on that old piece of junk, just imagine what it can do for my new car." By putting a product in the most difficult situation—giving it a task that seems impossible—you inject drama into the demonstration. Thus, when the product accomplishes a seemingly impossible task, the demonstration has the greatest impact upon the viewer.

An effective demonstration, however, doesn't have to be confined to one benefit. Because of time limitations, many advertisers are able to concentrate on only one product benefit, believing that trumpeting only the major selling point will have the greatest results. They ignore the many buyers interested in the product's secondary benefits. In the Nu-Finish spot, the product's multifaceted benefits are demonstrated. Not only is it shown working on old, dull finishes, shining brighter than competitive products, but also how it lasts through rains and washes. By spelling out these secondary benefits, a product is automatically made more attractive to a wider range of viewers.

Product solutions can also be demonstrated using the Parallel Structure Technique (PST). This involves placing the viewer in two identical situations: one with the product advertised and one without it. This parallel structure motivates the viewer to objectively analyze his need for the product. Consider the commercial for Tarn-X, a product that instantly dissolves tarnish from gold, silver, and copper. Using PST, the commercial begins by showing a woman confronted with a table overflowing with tarnished plates, utensils, and antiques. The scene cuts to the same setting, but this time the viewer sees the woman dip a tarnished spoon into Tarn-X, and when the spoon emerges it is shining. The before-and-after (parallel images) are burned into the viewer's mind, and the benefits of Tarn-X are made crystal clear.

Finally, there is no more powerful sales tool than a money-back guarantee. How often have you heard people say, "I buy at Marshall Field's because I know if I'm not satisfied, I get my money back." With all the benefits Field's can offer the consumer, their money-back guarantee is by far the one most responsible for bringing customers into their stores. Thus, it is ironic that so many advertisers take the highly motivational guarantee for granted. Perhaps they don't realize the paramount importance of a money-back guarantee in establishing a product's credibility. The money-back guarantee is especially significant when the product demonstration is so unbelievable or fantastic that the viewer might be skeptical about it. The guarantee bridges the credibility gap. It is the advertiser's promise to put his money where his mouth is, and that makes the offer difficult to ignore. For the viewer, treading the fine line between buying or not buying a product, the guarantee is the nudge he needs to cross that line and make a positive buying decision. Products such as Miracle White and Lestoil were established on double or triple money-back guarantees.

Many advertisers have also forgotten the importance of

certain words such as "amazing," "revolutionary," "new," and "incredible." They immediately trigger the viewer's interest because they are the verbal equivalents of exclamation points, adding force to the sales presentation. Of course, these words should be used with discretion. When a product is not "amazing," it would be inappropriate to use the word. But when a product increases your gas mileage substantially or makes mopping the floor an easy job, then "amazing" is not only appropriate but accurate.

Perhaps some advertisers refrain from using these "buzz words" because they feel they've been overused or seem like hyperbole. If that is the case, they are making a costly error. If they have a product that is intrinsically exciting, they should convey that excitement to the viewer. Buzz words are loaded with meaning; they automatically imply that a product is beneficial. Without these words, a commercial for an extraordinary product becomes ordinary.

Another rule for creating motivating commercials is: Supply the audience with enough information to make an educated buying decision. It is a rule that is consistently broken. How many times have you seen a commercial that has neglected to give essential information about a product? Information such as how it works, how much it costs, and where you can buy it. After viewing a noninformational commercial, the audience is left with many questions and no answers. Without those answers it is difficult to make a buying decision.

The dearth of information in commercials is based on an outmoded assumption: that store clerks will supply customers with all the information they need. Years ago, this assumption was valid. Before the advent of high-volume discount stores and chains, the majority of consumers shopped at ma-and-pa stores. Those stores had knowledgeable salespeople who provided their customers with accurate, in-depth information about a product. Even larger stores featured demonstrations of new products, and their salesmen had the time and expertise to help customers make educated buying decisions.

In recent years, however, ma-and-pa stores have gone

the way of the buffalo. If not quite extinct, they account for only a small percentage of total retail sales. The big discount stores get the biggest slice of the pie, and their clerks are either too busy or lack the ability to give customers accurate, detailed information about a product.

Thus, it is incumbent upon advertisers to "inform" consumers about their products in commercials. They must assume that there is no one in the store who can provide the essential facts about products. If advertisers have demonstrably beneficial products, why not show those benefits?

The information-filled commercial is a result of a "journalistic" approach to advertising. These commercials answer the who, what, why, when, and where about a product. Whom is the product for? What does it do? Why is it beneficial? When can it be used? Where can it be bought? If the product is a beneficial one, the more information given about it, the better . . . both for the consumer and the advertiser.

The type of commercial I have described in the preceding pages is one that can work for any product, providing that product has a demonstrable, unique, consumer benefit. The products can run the gamut, from cars to banks to soft drinks to credit cards. Let's examine a few product categories that usually don't use the "problem-solution" formula I've outlined, and explore what would happen if they did.

FOOD

Food advertising is a haven for animation, jingles, and slice-of-life techniques. For parity products, these techniques probably serve a purpose. But for food that has some demonstrable, unique benefit, information-filled commercials could be extremely beneficial. Food products that fall in this category are high-fiber cereals, unusual spices, salt and sugar substitutes, low-calorie desserts, and any other food or food-related products.

For instance, when an unusual frozen dinner is introduced via a television commercial, it can be strongly motivational. If it is frozen crêpes, it solves the problem of boring, bland, "chicken potpie-type" frozen dinners. It offers the solution of interesting, continental dining, and that is a benefit that can be demonstrated in a commercial.

BANKS

Financial institutions are bastions of generalized, image-oriented advertising. They infrequently spell out specific services that benefit the consumer. Instead, they rely on general "themes" such as "The Bank for Business" or "The Big Bank with the Little Bank Inside." Such themes are fine, but they would be far more motivating if they backed them up with specific, beneficial services.

A commercial for a bank should begin with a common problem: lack of courteous, personalized service. The bank's solution to that problem should then be demonstrated: tellers who greet customers by name, a bank "host" who meets customers when they enter and directs them to the proper area, etc. The benefits of becoming a customer of this bank are spelled out in compelling terms, and viewers are motivated to respond to the commercial.

CARS

Commercials for automobiles fall into what I like to call the "country roads rut." A sizable percentage of automobile advertising consists of long shots of cars traveling scenic country roads or medium shots of cars against breathtaking views (on mountaintops) or close-ups of cars with a beautiful woman draped over the hood in the middle of a field, or a car on top of a mountain. I have no idea what all this fresh air has to do with selling cars except for the production company that makes the commercial.

Dashboards are an extremely motivating part of auto sales. Yet, how often does an advertiser extol the virtues of his car's dash? Commercials convince people to buy cars by offering them a benefit: better gas mileage, lower price, spaciousness, good handling. Though some commercials advertising cars do consist of demonstrations ("We drove this car a hundred miles through the toughest terrain imaginable"), many do not. And, often, these demonstrations are not conducted so as to motivate the viewer. For instance, a commercial that demonstrates a car's excellent gas mileage cannot merely list that car's miles per gallon and show the car rolling along a stretch of road. It should clearly demonstrate how much money the consumer will save in a year if he buys the car that gets thirty miles per gallon as opposed to the car that gets fifteen miles per gallon.

Automobile advertisers are also guilty of committing a cardinal sin, one that other advertisers are guilty of. They tend to sell features, not benefits. And features cannot be equated with benefits! Too many car commercials emphasize features such as rack-and-pinion steering, dual carburetion, or independent suspension. These commercials operate under the false assumption that the mere mention of these features will help the viewer know what the hell they mean. In fact, most viewers have no idea what benefits any of these features generate. It is essential that the commercial translate those features into benefits; that the viewer be told that rack-and-pinion steering will give him better control and cornering ability; that dual carburetion will give him more acceleration and power; that independent suspension will give him a smoother, more comfortable ride.

Up until this point, I have concentrated on the content of a motivating commercial. But content is only one element in the creation of a commercial that creates sales. The "look" of the commercial is another element that must be considered. Here is a rule of thumb: The more "real" the commercial looks, the more believable it will be. Theoretically, commercials aired live have the greatest selling power. Realistically, live commercials are seldom done because of logistical problems. In the fifties, however, nothing better bridged the credibility gap than the live commercial. Because it was live, the viewer accepted what he was viewing:

a demonstration of a product could not be tampered with. Thus, what he saw was what he got.

Today, the next best thing to "live" is videotape. Unlike film, it has a quality of cinéma vérité. Videotape has a documentary feel to it, whereas film suggests fiction. Over the years, our agency has resisted the trend toward filmed commercials, relying on videotape because it makes a presentation more believable. An added bonus of videotape, of course, is that it is far less expensive to use, saving clients a great deal of money.

Benefit-oriented demonstration commercials should have a "live" feel to them. Television viewers have become increasingly sophisticated, attuned to the medium's ability to tamper with reality. They have built-in cynicism toward products that claim to do amazing things, and the only way to break through that cynicism is with a believable commercial.

Most people in the advertising world are aware of this cynicism. Some of them, however, make a crucial error in trying to combat it. For instance, some commercials attempt to simulate ridiculous "real life" situations—how often do a husband and wife argue about using a deodorant? How common is it for a secretary to tell her boss he has bad breath?

But "slice-of-life" commercials, even if they are true to life, are still distortions of reality. The viewer is aware that he is watching actors and actresses reciting rehearsed lines, and that awareness prevents the commercial from being as effective as it might be. For these commercials to work, they would have to invoke what Coleridge referred to as "suspension of disbelief"—the willingness of the reader (or viewer) to forget he is reading a book (or seeing a movie)—and approach it as if it were reality. While such a suspension of disbelief might work in literature or film, it won't work in a television commercial.

Which is not to say that all slice-of-life spots don't work. If they appear during a period of low sales resistance when the viewer's alertness level is down, it can make a positive impression. But if the commercial runs during a period of

high sales resistance, the alert viewer will instinctively analyze and reject the obviously "staged" slice-of-life situation.

Similarly, animation, fantasy, and humor are advertising
techniques that detract from a commercial's credibility. (Animation should be used only when a product demonstration
is physically impossible, such as fertilizer's ability to help
grass grow.) On the other hand, the "demonstration" approach can provide the credibility necessary for a viewer to
buy a product. A demonstration of a product is exactly what
it purports to be: there is no need for suspension of disbelief.

The final element necessary to create a motivating commercial is time. There is a general misconception that thirty
seconds is a commercial's optimum length. In fact, thirty
seconds is an arbitrary number with absolutely no relation to
the realities of selling products. It is the standard length of
commercials because that's how long it takes a second hand
to move halfway around a clock. To designate one specific
time as being best for all commercials is like saying all books
should be two hundred pages, all symphonies should be
forty-five minutes, and all movies should be ninety minutes.
By limiting commercials to thirty seconds, advertisers are
also limiting the amount of information they can convey
about a product. In many cases, the time limitation is unfair
to the potential customer; he just doesn't have enough information to make a buying decision.

To determine the length of a commercial, an advertiser
must determine how long it takes to sell his product. Generally, between one and two minutes is necessary to do an
effective selling job. Some products could easily use an
hour, but unfortunately FCC regulations limit advertisers to
two minutes.

An even more compelling reason for advertisers to create longer commercials is the isolation factor theory. It is the
result of six years of research, and it stipulates that if you can
obtain sole possession of a commercial break, you can
greatly increase the motivational power of your commercial.
By "isolating" the viewer, you allow him to make a buying
decision before he is distracted by other commercials.

To dominate a 120-second break, you must create a commercial at least 90 seconds in length; to own that break, your commercial must be the entire two minutes.

If you don't do either of these two things, you run the risk of irritating viewers by being within a cluster of four 30-second spots. When you gang up on the viewer with clusters, it is analogous to four or more salesmen confronting him at once . . . as soon as one stops talking, the next one starts. The customer cannot absorb the first pitch before the second salesman starts talking. The viewer's irritation level becomes so high he often rejects all the products being sold.

If, however, you isolate your commercial, you become the only salesman in the viewer's living room, greatly increasing the chances that he will make a positive buying decision.

To measure the effect of longer commercials on viewers, we conducted a series of tests in conjunction with TVB. In these tests, we showed panels of women sets of commercials. One set consisted of four 30-second spots, another set included one 60-second commercial and two 30-second ones, another featured one 30-second spot and two 10-second spots, and there were various other combinations. These sets were shown with one 2-minute commercial in order to compare responses toward longer versus shorter commercials. In each test, the panel found the shorter, clustered commercials more irritating than the longer one. We discovered that viewers don't time commercials; they count them. When people are irritated by a commercial, they never say. "Not another two-minute commercial!" Instead, they say, "Six goddamned commercials in a row!"

Of course, I don't propose that all commercials be two minutes in length. As I stated earlier, commercials should only be as long as it takes to effectively sell the product. If a product could be sold in thirty seconds, however, an advertiser would get better results if he bought an extra ninety seconds of "dead air" to isolate his thirty-second commercial.

If that sounds like a revolutionary proposal, consider that corporations such as Hallmark, Kraft Foods, and IBM sponsor "specials" precisely because it allows them to isolate longer commercials within these shows. And they have found that these commercials are extraordinarily effective in moving their products.

Any marketing or advertising executive reading this chapter should now be asking a very logical question: How much should a good commercial cost? The answer: Usually under $15,000. If that seems a ridiculously low figure, remember what inflates the price of commercials: film, jingles, elaborate productions, location shooting, a full cast of actors and actresses. By eliminating the show biz aspect of creating a commercial, you eliminate the major expenditures.

A top-quality, videotaped demonstration commercial should cost between $8,000 and $15,000 to produce. If you spend $100,000 more on production, chances are the aesthetics will be nicer but the results at point of sale will be the same. At the insistence of a client, we have upgraded a $12,000 commercial to $100,000. The client got a very warm feeling on the inside, but the sales remained the same on the outside.

The wise advertiser spends time rather than money to ensure the success of his advertising. Admittedly, it takes many hours to create a motivating commercial. But as the sales figures come in, it will prove to be time well spent.

12

How to Buy
Sales-Producing
TV Time at
Bargain Basement
Rates

**EICOFF'S LAW: The price of an advertising medium will
increase until such a time as it will no longer pay out
for the advertiser . . . at which point the advertiser will
quit using it.**

A common misconception among many print advertisers
(and some broadcast advertisers as well!) is that television is
a prohibitively expensive advertising medium. They see the
rates for prime-time shows as high as $150,000 for thirty
seconds and shudder. Yet, would they shudder if they knew
they could buy two minutes of TV time in a major market for
under $200?

The problem, quite simply, is one of perspective. If advertisers view prime time as the only time worth buying,
many, of course, are going to find the rates out of their
ballpark. But that is like looking at a magazine and believing
the back cover is the only worthwhile space for their ads.

As I have explained in previous chapters, prime time is
not the best slot for benefit-oriented, demonstration commercials. Therefore, my discussion of media buying will per-
tain to that huge silent majority of time that is not prime. For
any individual or company with a unique, beneficial product,
it is the most valuable TV time that exists.

At this point, you might be wondering why I am limiting this discussion to television. What about print? The answer is complex, but bear with me while I explain it.

Television is the greatest medium ever conceived. It is the only truly egalitarian medium, reaching the young and old, the rich and poor, the literate and the illiterate, the wise man and the fool. Nothing can rival its immediacy, its ability to stimulate so many of the senses. It offers so much to so many that it cannot help but evoke an emotional and/or intellectual response from millions of Americans every second of every day.

Yet with all this power, television is still tremendously insecure. This insecurity manifests itself in its liberal credit policies. Virtually anyone can walk in off the street and a television station will give him credit. The stations seldom ask for financial statements or references. Although television stations continue to suffer tremendous credit losses, few have done anything to alleviate the problem.

On the other hand, the print medium is not only quite strict about credit but offers cash discounts for prompt payment, and exacts penalties if payment is late. Usually they allow a 2 percent discount for payment by the tenth of each month, and some disallow the 15 percent agency commission if payment is not received by the fifteenth of the month . . . five days later. Because television stations tolerate sixty-to-ninety-day payment delays, advertisers frequently use TV's money to pay other media.

One of the most blatant examples of the television industry's insecurity is its total disregard for rate cards.

Virtually every television station, big or small, network or independent, has a hundred different rates for a hundred different advertisers. Because of this willingness to wheel and deal, they have chosen to live on what I call the "Avenue of Harlots."

Recently, a Fortune 500 company's invoice for a thirty-second spot on a New York TV station was sent to us by mistake. This company was paying $1,380 for a 30-second spot on the same night and in the same show we were paying $175 for a 120-second spot.

Another company's invoice sent to us in error shows a prime 30-second spot on a California station listed at $400 on their card. This company was paying $270 (about 33 percent off). We were buying a 120-second spot in the same show on the same night for $75.

Television's insecurity is responsible for this situation. From my experience, it seems that this insecurity stems from the very nature of its product. It is a perishable one; if a time slot goes by unbought, it is revenue lost. Such impermanence naturally leads to insecurity.

Yet this very insecurity is what makes television a potential gold mine for the savvy advertiser. The advertiser's media-buying service or agency, if they are knowledgeable and skilled, should consistently buy time at "bottom quarter" rates. If a station offers a hundred different rates to a hundred different advertisers, the effective media buyer should be able to obtain rates that fall in the bottom quadrant of rates offered.

Unfortunately, many agencies are unable to do this. Their media-buying departments are hamstrung by tradition—a tradition that locks media buyers into a rigid pattern of buys. For instance, a client will notify his agency that he wants a specific number of rating points in specific markets over a specific period of time: 200 rating points in fifty top markets over thirteen weeks. This method of buying is tantamount to demanding the agency "rip off" the client. A good media buyer, given room to negotiate, can actually buy 200 rating points in New York or Chicago for less than it takes to buy the same number of points in Houston or Phoenix. A sharp buyer can do this because stations in larger markets are more willing to wheel and deal than stations in smaller markets; larger-market stations are more willing to slash rates if they do a lot of business with an agency.

However, as I said, the very method set forth by the client bars the media buyer from taking advantage of these low rates. Tell a client he is paying more for television time in Houston than New York and he'll explode. He can't understand why he pays more for the smaller market.

And the agency, aware of this inequity, not only doesn't

negotiate the lowest rates to prevent the problem, but also keeps the rates in line to avoid cutting their 15 percent agency commission income. Obviously, the more of the client's money they spend on the media, the more commission they earn. Thus, the standard operating procedure at nearly all agencies is to fight for enough discount to meet the client criteria.

The most effective procedure would be for the client to give the agency a budget based on a reasonable cost per thousand along with a minimum "rating-point level" for each market. An advertiser could then tell its agency to spend the full budget, while giving them the freedom and incentive to obtain the maximum number of rating points within the budget. Implicit in this arrangement is that the agency will not be penalized for buying the greatest number of points at the lowest possible cost.

Rating points, however, should not be the be-all and end-all of media buying (or even the major criterion). At best, rating points should serve only as a guide for buyers. At worst, they can lead buyers down the path to disaster. Rating points are simply a percentage of the total homes in a given market. If a market has 100,000 homes, one rating point equals 1,000 homes. This 1,000 homes per point holds true if the point occurs at 9 A.M. or 9 P.M., at noon or midnight.

The reason advertisers pay premium prices for prime-time buys is that prime-time shows offer greater reach . . . that is, the highest number of unduplicated homes. A little arithmetic, however, demonstrates the fallacy in that reasoning. Prime time generally costs anywhere from five to ten times per point as much as fringe time. If you spend the same amount of money in fringe that you would in prime, your cume (the number of people reached multiplied by the number of times they are reached) will be at least four to five times as great. Thus, non-prime time offers advertisers the best value for the money they spend.

Late-night television often gives advertisers the best return for their money. Most agencies refuse to believe that.

Perhaps their negative attitude toward late-night advertising is ingrained, a misconception that has been handed down from one generation of advertisers to the next. In the late forties, when ratings were determined by random phone calls, there were no ratings after 11 P.M or before 8 A.M. Thus, the standard belief was: where there are no ratings, there is no audience. Today, there are no official ratings for shows after 1:30 A.M.; thus, in the eyes of most media buyers, the time is worthless. However, a number of special ratings have been commissioned for this late-night time period, and they show that some stations received ratings in the 4–6 range, which compares favorably with many prime access shows.

In addition, the fact is that certain advertisers, particularly car dealers, find that this time is most productive for them. One reason for late-night advertising's effectiveness is that the advertiser often has a captive audience. In many cities, there is only one station with programming after 1:30 A.M., Those watching TV watch that station regardless of programming . . . in effect, "it's the only game in town."

The traditional method of media buying also pits agency buyer against station seller. This very buying concept is counterproductive to good media selection. Station representatives and personnel call on an agency for the sole purpose of selling time. Once they have accomplished that—once they walk out with a contract in hand—they feel their job is over. Whether the commercial succeeds or fails to move the merchandise off the shelf at a profitable level is of little concern to the station rep.

This tradition has been maintained by agencies that put a desk between media buyer and seller. They keep the media seller totally ignorant of the marketing strategies and goals of their clients.

To ensure effective media buying, this concept must be scrapped. The buyer and seller must become part of the same team. The agency must convince the station representative that he has a greater stake in the success of the campaign than the agency! If that seems a difficult proposition to understand, consider that the station gets 85 percent of an advertiser's expenditures, and the agency gets only 15 percent. As long as the commercial continues to successfully sell the product, the advertiser will renew and renew the schedule. If it isn't successful, the income stops! The game is over! The agency and the station lose. Therefore, it is incumbent upon the station rep to do whatever he can to ensure that commercial's success, even to the extent of offering better times at lower rates, free spots, or merchandising help.

And make no mistake about it, a station rep can do many things to ensure that success. He is the one who determines the specific time, show, and rate for the commercial. If he is convinced he has a vested interest in giving the media buyer the best time, show, and rate, the advertising will be infinitely more effective.

Many agencies will say this arrangement is impossible. They'll explain that they don't expect their advertising to show any immediate measurable results, and, therefore, schedules aren't renewed based on sales.

For agencies that subscribe to "investment spending," the "team" approach is indeed impossible. But for an agency with its sights set upon immediate measurable sales, the team approach is not only possible, it is practical. If, for instance, an agency employs a Key Outlet strategy for its client, those outlets can furnish the agency with a week-to-week statement of sales for the client's product. Thus, the effect of the program can be easily evaluated. The station rep is made aware of the agency's ability to measure results, and the rep is willing to do everything within his power to ensure the success of the commercial.

On the other side of the fence, the media buyer must become more than a functionary. Too often, the media buyer is looked upon as nothing more than a robot that executes the commands of the computer. The good media buyer, however, is responsible for a great part of the success of any product. He (or she) has a keen marketing mind as well as a thorough understanding of media and how they work. He can deal directly with the client, evaluating results, recommending changes, and fulfilling the function of an account executive. The perspicacious agency will recognize its media buyers' talents and, instead of promoting them out of the job they do best, will keep them there by offering monetary incentives and increased job responsibility so the agency can best utilize their valuable skills.

The key to successful media buying is flexibility. By arbitrarily predetermining media schedules, you are locking a client into a media cell from which there is no escape. The length of a schedule should vary according to product and market. Every market must be viewed as a profit center. Many agencies attempt to secure distribution in virtually every market no matter what the cost. They refuse to bow to the realities of a bad market, plowing more and more of a client's money into markets where the product isn't selling in an attempt to maintan the product in those markets. A flexible media buyer, however, will recognize that certain markets—for whatever reasons—are death for certain products. They will yank the plug from that market's media and let the client's competition get its brains knocked out by the market's natural resistance to that product category.

Finally, there is the Hills and Valleys theory of media buying. Every television station in the country has busy periods (hills) and slow periods (valleys).

The unsophisticated media buyer attempts to climb those hills, buying time when time is scarce and rates are high. The sophisticated media buyer, on the other hand, looks for the fertile valleys where time is plentiful and most effective in moving merchandise off the shelves. (Seasonal conditions, of course, can affect this buying method and adjustments can be made in such instances.) If the media buyer and station rep are working together to make a product a success, they will have more freedom to plan an effective media strategy in these valleys.

The theory of sales resistance (discussed in chapter 5) should be the guiding light for all media buys. It provides the parameters (early morning, late evening, and weekends)

SEASONAL DIRECT RETURN CURVE

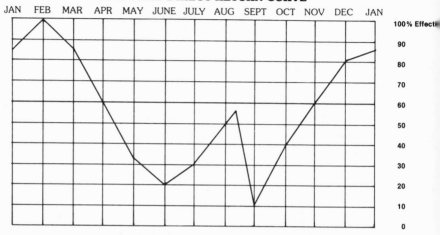

within which the media buyer will find times when the viewer is least resistant to a motivating commercial. The isolation factor theory (discussed in chapter 11) also is of crucial importance for the media buyer. Keeping this thoery in mind, a media buyer will attempt to dominate commercial breaks rather than be caught in a cluster.

This chapter, of course, is more than a series of theories. My agency has put these concepts into practice and found them to be quite workable. In fact, a number of major agencies have begun incorporating facets of this media-buying philosophy to increase the cost-efficiency and effectiveness of their media departments.

Despite this, most media-buying departments and agencies remain hopelessly mired in outdated media-buying techniques. Large agencies often promote their best buyers into oblivion. As soon as a media buyer is recognized as skillful, he is immediately promoted to media director or an account executive and is relieved of the everyday, so-called menial task of media buying.

Agencies and their advertisers must reevaluate both the role of the media buyer and their approach toward media buying to increase the effectiveness of their advertising. If they do not, they will continue to pay increasingly higher rates for decreasingly effective campaigns.

13

How to Make a Million-Dollar Idea Worth a Million Bucks

I know a man who wrote a book called "How to Make a Million Dollars in the Mail Order Business." He made a million dollars offering the book for sale by running mail-order ads in numerous publications. The book suggested that you write a book called "How to Make a Million Dollars in the Mail Order Business."

Before there was the plastic sandwich bag, the disposable razor, and the electric toothbrush, there were the ideas for all those products. And in most cases, the people who had those ideas never acted on them. They let someone else come up with the idea and make a fortune from it. It's not unusual to be walking through a store or watching television and see a new product that you invented in your mind years ago. You smack yourself on the head and ask "Why didn't I do something about it?"

The answer is that you didn't know what to do. For the average person, the process of translating a product idea into reality seems to require a prohibitive amount of money, resources, and knowledge. (The industrial manufacturer, too, is reluctant to venture into the consumer marketplace because he feels he lacks the expertise or personnel to make that venture work.) Of course, when you first think of that wonderful product, you are too wrapped up in the power and glory of the IDEA to worry about actually making it work. You cloak the idea in the fabric of fantasy, imagining the fame and riches it will bring you. Instead of doing something about the idea, you think it to death. The product idea, once an indelible image in your mind, fades like an old photograph. The real problems of manufacturing, marketing, and advertising it keep the idea imprisoned in your head, and eventually it disappears. The next time you think of it is when you see YOUR IDEA as somebody else's product.

I grimace every time somebody tells me a story like this, and, believe me, I've heard infinite variations on this same theme. To avoid hearing any more of those stories, I will now give you a do-it-yourself kit that contains instructions on how to build a successful product from scratch.

First, let us begin with the idea. You must objectively determine whether it is a viable one. I stress the word "objectively" because you tend to fall in love with your idea to the exclusion of any rational analysis of it. To prevent this, here is a checklist to use in analyzing your product idea.

1. Can you sell the product for at least three and a half times what it cost you to make and package?

2. Does it have wide appeal? Does the product's potential audience cut across class, ethnic, and age lines? If your audience is limited, so is the potential of your product. A product that makes delicious matzah ball soup is good. If it can make matzah ball soup and potato pancakes, even better. But if it can make matzah ball soup, donuts, and applesauce, then you've got a winner. The more universal the problems your product solves, the greater the chances for success.

3. Is the product unique? "Unique" is a word subject to interpretation. Obviously, by "unique" I don't mean that the product has to be on the level of a hair restorer or a new energy source. In one sense, "unique" simply means that the product can do something better than competitive products, or—and this is relatively rare—it opens up a new product category.

But uniqueness can apply to a "tangential" aspect of the product. It might apply to a new package design for an old product. Shaving cream was around for a long time before somebody thought of taking it out of a tube and putting it in an aerosol can. And many people were selling records before we hit upon the scheme of packaging top hits of a specific era (big bands, fifties rock, etc.) and putting them on one album. A classic example of a recent, unique package design for an old product is putting soap in a liquid dispenser; or turning a cassette player and a pair of earphones into a portable private stereo system.

Another area that can be unique is price. If you can sell an old product at a new price—either higher or lower—you've distinguished your product from others. To sell a product at a lower price—a color TV for $99, for instance—usually requires a technological innovation that allows you to manufacture the product for far less than it normally costs. But if you are savvy and daring enough, you might be able to raise the price of a product and reach a formerly unreachable audience. Polyglycoat used this strategy successfully. By offering their car protection at an inflated price, Polyglycoat was perceived by the public as a necessary, albeit expensive, purchase to protect a car's finish. Or you might take a toothpaste, call it Topol, position it as the "smoker's toothpaste," give it a hefty $5.00 price tag, and thus carve out a whole new market.

Finally, an old product will be perceived as unique if its unique selling proposition is changed. We did this very thing with a product called Dark Eyes. It had enjoyed only a small success as an eyebrow tint for female swimmers. But when we created a commercial that positioned the product as the "30-day eye make-up," sales skyrocketed.

4. Can the product's benefit be graphically demonstrated? One must evaluate a product idea in terms of advertising—how would the product look in a television commercial? If it lends itself to a step-by-step demonstration of how the product actually can benefit the consumer, it will have a lot going for it. Having a terrific product doesn't necessarily guarantee its success. A product benefit might be an esoteric one that is not easily demonstrated. For instance,

someone might invent a filter that actually enhances the flavor of coffee, yet that would be an extraordinarily difficult thing to illustrate. A product that can be demonstrated, however, immediately activates one or more of the senses. Our Roll-O-Matic mop commercial automatically activated the viewers' sense of touch—with a flick of a switch, the pain and strain of mopping floors was eliminated before their very eyes.

5. Determine whether you can sell the product at a reasonable price. While the previous four points are important, markup is essential. A fatal mistake many neophyte businessmen make is underpricing their product and not allowing for a decent profit margin. With virtually any product, this rule-of-thumb should be followed: there should be a minimum three-and-a-half times markup from the actual cost of merchandise in package to retail selling price. Notice that I have used the word "minimum." That is because a product can be marked up ten or twenty times, depending on what it does. It is essential to remember that a product's worth is measured by the job it performs—if it has a high perceived value, it should have a high price tag. When we handled a hair-cutting device, we advised the client to sell it for a much higher price than he initially wanted to. The reason: by giving yourself one haircut, you automatically saved four dollars at the very least. Ultimately the product would save a customer hundreds of dollars, making its perceived value quite high. The fact that it cost very little to manufacture, therefore, had no bearing on how it was priced.

Once you have run your product idea through this gauntlet—and if it has survived—the next step is to plan a marketing and advertising strategy. If you happen to have an extra million dollars or so lying around, then you can contact a major advertising agency to plan a multimedia program for your product, arrange for distribution in stores throughout the country, set up "focus groups" and "theoretical research studies," and spend months developing a strategy. If, however, you are not heir to some vast fortune, or if you don't believe in squandering your time and money needlessly, there are other options.

One option that is available is going to a firm that helps people market their inventions. On the surface, this appears to be an attractive option. You've seen ads promising inventors the moon, and it's easy to be hooked on those promises. But in most cases, these firms only offer promises, with little of substance to back them up. What usually happens is this: you bring your prototype or product idea in, and the marketing director of the "Inventions" company cannot contain his enthusiasm, telling you your product has great potential. Then he hits you with the bill for his enthusiasm: around $1,500 to $2,500. For that sum, he tells you he'll send out a fleet of salesmen to major companies throughout the country to peddle the product. In fact, they will do nothing of the kind. At best, they will spend a couple hundred dollars of your money on a feeble attempt at getting the product marketed, and pocket the rest. Most of these invention companies are fraudulent, and you can tell they are frauds as soon as they ask for your money. Any reputable firm would be willing to market your product for a piece of the action, for that is where the real money is to be made. If you do bring your product to one of those invention-marketing firms, test them by asking this simple question: What products have you successfully marketed? If they can name five—and they check out—then they are probably sincere and trustworthy. If they don't come up with a satisfactory answer, however, walk out the door . . . fast!

Another option you have is to walk in the door of an advertising agency. And, of course, not just any agency will do. Big agencies probably won't give you the time of day. What you must search for is an agency with a proven track record; an agency that is savvy and skilled enough to bring your product into the marketplace in an effective, cost-efficient manner. Those agencies are difficult to find, but they do exist. Once you've found an agency you're comfortable with, a major decision has to be made.

That decision is whether your product is suitable for direct response, retail, or any other marketing direction.

Once again, let us define our terms. Direct response means simply that you offer consumers a product they can order via phone or mail. The commercial or ad contains a toll-free number and mailing address. The product is not available in any stores. There are two subdivisions of retail marketing: (1) Key Outlet—the commercial offers consumers a product that is available only in certain stores, which are tagged at the end of the commercial; (2) universal distribution—the product is available in all stores.

A number of factors must be weighed before choosing a marketing approach. Certain products automatically fall into the direct-response category: book and record clubs, insurance, fund-raising organizations, and any product involving sets for continuous shipment. You cannot sell them through normal retail channels. But that doesn't mean that everything else is destined for retail marketing. Often, retail products get their start in direct response. Direct response provides the most cost-efficient forum for test marketing. For about $12,000–$15,000 including the commercial and time, virtually any product can be tested.

Direct response, implemented properly, is virtually a foolproof testing method for any product. It gives the product the benefit of the doubt: you must choose the best market, the best stations, and the best times to run the test. Thus, if the test doesn't work under these conditions, it will never work. If it does work, the test is expanded gradually to other markets, and expansion to new markets is actually financed by success in previous markets. Often, a successful direct-response product can be channeled into Key Outlet Marketing, and eventually into universal distribution.

From my discussion of Key Outlet Marketing in chapter 7, you should have a basic grasp of what it entails and how it is distinct from any other kind of retail advertising. But no matter how carefully I have explained Key Outlet Marketing in theory, the story is not complete until I explain how it actually works in practice. So here is a textbook example of what happens when you've brought your product idea to the threshold of success and decide to test the Key Outlet Marketing waters.

Begin with a product that we will call KOM-1. The selling price of KOM-1 is pegged at $10.00. Thirty percent of that—$3.00—goes to the chains, leaving you with $7.00. Next, factor in the following expenses: $2.00 for actual cost of goods, 50 cents for actual freight, 42 cents (6 percent) for administration, 70 cents (10 percent) for sales cost. Then, you must determine the absolute minimum profit you would accept for your capital investment. You decide upon $1.00 as that minimum profit. Deduct all the aforementioned numbers from $7.00 and you end up with $2.38. That $2.38 is what we call the "magic number." If your advertising costs stay around that number, everything works like magic.

Next, choose two markets for test marketing. We have certain markets that we use almost exclusively for tests. They include Portland, New Orleans, Sacramento, San Diego, Orlando, and Louisville. All these cities have certain things in common: excellent retail chains our agency has established a working relationship with, television stations where we can make excellent media buys, and a history of getting full cooperation from everyone. In addition, all these markets rate 100 on the Product Marketing Index (PMI).

The PMI was developed years ago by our agency as a tool to differentiate one market from another. Of course, that violates the normal test procedures in advertising, which often select "average" markets for tests.

Individual markets vary just as individual people do. That is why the PMI came into existence. Some markets such as Chicago, Detroit, and New York have index numbers above 100, while others have numbers below 100. The index, however, uses 100 as a base number; it tells you that for X number of advertising dollars, you can move 100 units in a 100-indexed market. But if you spend the same amount in a 115-indexed market, you will move an additional 15 units. This index is based on a normal universal product, and is accurate to within 5 percent either way. And, obviously, it is of incalculable value in helping a client budget his advertising expenditures.

The PMI was developed by factoring in such things as

the number of TV stations in a market, the rates of those stations, the strength of the Key Outlets, and the results of thousands of tests run in those markets. The only time the PMI has to be adjusted is for seasonally, geographically, or regionally oriented products. To use an extreme example, a snow shovel cannot be plugged into the PMI for New Orleans because snowfall there is minimal; or, you can't use the PMI of Atlanta for grits, as the use of the product there would be far greater per capita than for San Diego.

Now, let us go back to KOM-1 and our magic number, which was $2.38. We decide to test it in Portland and Louisville, 100-indexed markets. We also decide to spend $4,500 in a three-week campaign in each market. The next step is to take $2.38 and divide it into $4,500. The result is 1,890. Thus, we have to sell 1,890 units in each market in the three-week test to reach the magic number. Of course, it is rare to hit the magic number on the nose. To cover ourselves in case we sell more than expected, we stock the stores with approximately one and a half times what we need to reach the magic number. In this instance, that means 2,850 units per market.

The commercial airs, and four things can happen.

1. We sell all 2,850 units in the markets which means our advertising allowance (the magic number) is too high, and we must compensate by increasing the amount of product in the market. Because the test was successful, we then expand to five "upgraded" markets—markets with slightly higher PMI numbers. If those five markets continue to work for the product, we continue to expand, always limiting the expansion to five upgraded markets. We have found that five markets allows for a good profit while still ensuring that if the product doesn't sell in the new markets, the losses will be minimal.

2. We sell about 1,890 units, thus hitting the magic number. We reschedule advertising, resupply the market, and expand according to number one.

3. We sell about 1,600 units. If this occurs, we'll give the product the benefit of the doubt because it has come

reasonably close to the magic number. We'll allow the product to remain in the stores for several weeks to see if we move the necessary 1,890 units. Because we are so close to success, we reexamine our packaging, TV commercials, media selection, hoping we can improve them to produce the needed additional sales.

4. The product "bombs." Though this happens infrequently, it does happen, and we try to defuse the bomb before it does any more damage. We'll give the client a choice: he can either let us reexamine the commercial and see if we can improve it and run another test or he can take his losses and get out of the market. It is unprecedented for an agency to even suggest to a client that a product might be a failure, but that is what we do if the test doesn't work.

(We are often asked why we chose a 100-PMI market when we could have chosen 115-PMI markets. The answer is that the higher PMI markets are far more costly. For example, it costs $4,500 to test a 100-PMI market, but $24,000 to test New York City, Chicago, or Los Angeles. We test the less expensive markets to hold down the client's risk factor.)

If you follow the steps outlined in this chapter, I would estimate your chances for success at 90 percent. Ninety percent because that has been our agency's success rate with new product introductions. Any agency worth its billings should be able to guarantee you a similar success rate if they are cognizant of the strategies I've discussed.

Marketing and advertising a product is analogous to a poker game—the stakes are high and you're taking a gamble. But if you plan the game well, it's very difficult to lose. And if you stack the deck with aces and make sure you get your fair share of them, it's almost impossible to lose. Let's go over some of your aces.

First, you have the sales resistance theory working for you. Your commercial will air at a time when the viewer is most receptive to the commercial—when his conscious mind is least likely to screen out the message. Thus, you have a natural advantage over those still enamored by prime time.

Second, you have the isolation factor in your favor. As discussed in chapter 11, the isolation factor involves buying a block of time sufficient to dominate the commercial break—the viewer will see only one 2-minute spot instead of being battered by four 30-second spots. Our research shows that viewers respond more positively to one long commercial "isolated" during a show than a number of shorter commercials, which are irritating to viewers.

Third, your commercial will be distinctive. Unlike other commercials, which are created to win awards, boost egos, justify theoretical research or score well on "awareness" tests, yours has only one purpose: to sell the product. Everything that goes into the commercial—from creative to actual production—adheres to that purpose. For instance, use videotape rather than film, not because it will save you money (though that is a pleasant benefit), but because it gives the commercial the feel of cinéma vérité. Anything filmed is, by definition, one step removed from reality. It has a gauzy, slightly artificial "feel" to it—it connotes fiction, not fact. Videotape, on the other hand, has a documentary "feel." Consequently, when a product is demonstrated on videotape, the demonstration is rendered more credible. The viewer tends to believe in what he is seeing; he is not constantly reminded by the film's intrinsic "artificial" look that the demonstration has been staged. The result is a commercial that is unique and calls attention to itself because of that uniqueness.

Fourth, Key Outlet Marketing confers high visibility on any product. Because the chains that sell the Key Outlet product have a vested interest in it, they always give it the best and biggest display space in their stores. Shoppers in those stores—whether they've seen your commercial or not—cannot help but see your product.

Those are the four aces you should be holding. Perhaps you aren't playing the game by the rules. But if you can't afford to make a foolish bet, you've cut the odds down considerably. In fact, if you have a million-dollar idea for the ante, you can get in a pretty lucrative game.

14

Some of My Best Friends Are Entrepreneurs

What does it take to be a successful entrepreneur? Some say luck. Others say brains. Still others say money. I say you need none of those things.

What you do need is an inferiority complex, guts, intuition, and the ability to do what everyone says can't be done.

Before I explain those four entrepreneurial ingredients, let me issue a word of caution: the potential rewards of being an entrepreneur are more than equaled by the potential dangers. For every entrepreneur who found fame and fortune, there are ten who found nothing but anonymity and bankruptcy.

The idea of being an entrepreneur is seductive. Who is not enticed by the notion of being your own boss, of being totally responsible for your success or failure? We live in a society that deifies enormously successful entrepreneurs. Men such as William Randolph Hearst, Henry Ford, Howard Hughes, and Samuel Goldwyn have become legends. Books are written about them, and movies are made based on their lives.

"Caution" is the one word missing from these entrepreneurs' vocabularies. I think of the super-rich entrepreneurs I have known and caution has no place in their successes. I'm talking about men such as Senator Leblanc, founder of Hadacall; Sam Popeil, founder of Popeil Brothers; Abe Plough, founder of Plough, Inc.; Charlie Revson, founder of Revlon; Leonard Lavin, founder of Alberto Culver, Nieson Harris, creator of Toni home permanent; H. Leslie Atlass, one of the founders of CBS; Morry Goldblatt, founder of Goldblatt's; Norman Stone, founder of Stone Container; Leonard Rosen, founder of Gulf American; Bernie Mitchell, founder of Jovan; Marty Himmel, founder of Topol and Porcelana, among other products; John McArthur of Bankers Life and Casualty; Leo Singer, founder of Miracle White; Charlie Lubin, founder of the Kitchens of Sara Lee; Joe Cossman, direct marketing genius; Lee Ratner, founder of d-Con and Lehigh Acres, Florida; Leo Burnett, of Leo Burnett ad agency; Ted Turner, founder of Turner Enterprises, WTBS (Atlanta), owner of Atlanta Braves; Sam Rautbord, founder of Apeco. There are many I didn't know personally but who fall into the category of self-made entrepreneurs. Abe Pritzker, founder of numerous enterprises including Hyatt and the Cory Coffee Service concept; Michael Todd of movie fame; W. Clement Stone of Combined Insurance Company of America; Hugh Hefner, William Zeckendorf, and Arthur Rubloff of real estate fame.

Looking over this roll call of entrepreneurs, I find that their total net worth would surpass that of many industrialized European countries. Yet money is not what motivated their careers. Rather, it is the natural by-product of being an entrepreneur. Looking for a common thread that binds these men together at first seems difficult. They made their fortunes in different fields—some in advertising, some in broadcasting, some in manufacturing, some in real estate. Their personalities, too, varied.

But they all had four common characteristics that made them extraordinarily successful entrepreneurs. First, they had severe inferiority complexes. Because of this, they constantly were trying to prove themselves day by day, to show their friends, family, and business associates that they could succeed. The inferiority complex is insatiable—feed it one success and that only whets its appetite for the next one. This complex fuels the entrepreneur's drive. He constantly strives to overcome obstacles, no matter how large they might be. He is not content with making a million dollars, but desires to multiply that figure ad infinitum to accumulate more than he needs in ten lifetimes. When he adds millions to his assets, it doesn't change his life-style one iota. No matter how successful he becomes, the inferiority complex is always there, telling him that he must prove himself again today.

On the other hand, the superiority complex and entrepreneurs don't mix. A person who feels superior feels the world owes him a living, and that attitude will curtail the intensive drive the highly successful entrepreneur needs.

The second ingredient is "guts." I am not necessarily referring to physical courage but rather to a willingness to take outlandish risks for anything he believes in. Often, these risks entail money, his family, or security. Lee Ratner, for example, was willing to hock everything he owned (and some things he didn't) to make d-Con a success. An entrepreneur has to gamble! And often, the odds of that gamble paying off seem poor. But he will throw common sense and security out the window, mortgage the house, the car, and the family jewels and proceed to invest in that something he believes in. He rushes in where wise men fear to tread.

And that brings up the third essential ingredient: intuition. Entrepreneurs not only have the guts to gamble, but they know intuitively what to gamble on. Often this intuition defies reason. This intuition is almost a sixth sense; they come by it naturally. It is not something that can be taught or acquired through diligent study. For example, how did Bernie Mitchell know that the public would buy a low-priced, American-made fragrance when everyone said you can't sell a cheap American perfume—especially in an orange package. And years ago, John McArthur was considered a fool to introduce hospital insurance when everyone said nobody would buy "hospital" insurance. Intuition allowed these men to do "foolish" things. In the final analysis, the entrepreneur does not depend on market research or cost-analysis studies for his success. He depends on his own gut feelings, and if they are right—and most often they are—they make him richer and richer.

At this point, I should note that intuition is not necessarily synonymous with intelligence. In fact, most of the super-rich entrepreneurs I have mentioned do not have enormously high IQ's or even a great deal of formal education. For an entrepreneur, education can often do more harm than good. Thus, excessive amounts of education can be hazardous to a businessman's financial health. An MBA can cloud an entrepreneur's mind, filling it with equations and theories that make him wary of following his instincts. If an attractive business venture does not work within the formula taught in a business school, the MBA might shy away from it because the textbook says it won't work. The people who write those textbooks, however, usually aren't entrepreneurs.

The final ingredient in the formula is "being unaware of what one can't do." Henry Ford was told he couldn't mass-produce an automobile. Marty Himmel was told no one would pay five dollars a tube for toothpaste. Abe Plough was told that there was no market for children's aspirin. Sam Rautbord was told no one would spend hundreds of dollars for a photocopying machine as long as carbon paper was so inexpensive. These super-rich entrepreneurs were told by experts that their ideas couldn't possibly succeed. Yet the entrepreneurs refused to heed these warnings; common sense would have caused them to junk their concepts.

The entrepreneur does not know what he cannot do because he has imagination. If a market doesn't exist for a product, the entrepreneur imagines a way to create the market. If a business venture seems impossible, he does the impossible. The entrepreneur first creates a successful business enterprise in his mind, and then he translates it into reality.

But how important is luck in all of this? What about making the right connection? If you have the four ingredients I've discussed, luck and connections are relatively unimportant. Take every dollar from a true entrepreneur this week and next year he'll be rich again.

Most of the super-rich entrepreneurs have made and lost many fortunes during their short lifetimes. There is a perfect analogy: If you cut a worm in half, it will eventually grow whole again. This process of regeneration is as natural to the entrepreneur as it is to the worm.

There is one final question: Given the realities of the 1980s, can an entrepreneur with these four basic ingredients achieve the fame and fortune that was possible in the nineteenth and twentieth centuries? That is to say, is it likely that one can overcome the obstacles of overregulation by the federal government and the stranglehold big business has on most industries?

I believe that more opportunities exist today for the entrepreneur than ever before. For one thing, the Reagan administration is in the process of removing many of the regulations that have hampered small businessmen and decreasing (or eliminating) the power of agencies that enforce those regulations. More important, large corporations have become such huge bureaucracies that the entrepreneur can carve out new markets underneath those corporations' noses before they can respond. Because big business is so large, it tends to slowly respond to a market rather than create one. Because the big business executive spends 85 percent of his time protecting his job and only 15 percent doing it, big business tests, retests, and retests again any new product concept or service before a consensus is reached to mass-market it for fear a loser may cost some executive his job. On the other hand, the entrepreneur is not bound by bureaucratic red tape and can act swiftly and decisively.

For example, Minnetonka, Inc. was founded with operating capital of only $3,000. When they introduced Softsoap in twelve test markets, they generated $12 million in sales and carved out a market before Lever Brothers and Procter & Gamble knew what hit them.

Any entrepreneur with an inferiority complex, guts, intuition, and the ability to be unaware of what can't be done can achieve success today equal or greater than ever before.

15

How to Plug into Cable's Profit Source

Th;slie kiinek., jfiiosk jkls, jklieklslim kllsli, keliieu illiiel,. kkuuiope½perhlslm kdip '.-d ½ielliukellll's½p kelj.

That, in a few words, is the condition of cable at this writing! Trying to decipher the enormously complex, constantly changing cable situation is like trying to read an unknown language—parts of it might seem familiar, but it's difficult to make sense of the whole thing.

In this chapter, I will translate the strange language of cable. I will not write an all-encompassing, minutely detailed exegesis on the subject (that would be another book in and of itself). What I will do is define the most important terms and then discuss how cable can be used most profitably by the advertiser, the agency, the entrepreneur, and the consumer.

Literally translated, cable is simply a piece of wire that attaches to a television set and delivers something the set wouldn't have without that piece of wire. It might be better reception or a complete selection of alternative program selections. It could be four one-time spectaculars, or it could be a mere decoder. Originally, cable was merely an attachment from a master antenna to improve reception of local stations or to possibly pick up an additional station or two within a 100-mile radius.

When booster stations appeared, that radius grew to 300 to 400 miles, and translators brought in stations 1,000 miles away.

With the advent of paid cable, the situation changed. For a fee, the consumer could receive additional programming, which might include a choice of one or more sporting events not normally telecast on a regular channel. The paid cable concept then broadened, allowing subscribers to receive specialized programming—twenty-four-hour news, programming from superstations, concerts, and championship fights.

Presently, very few advertising agencies are taking advantage of what cable has to offer. They are reluctant to do so primarily because the major rating services do not have ratings for cable stations. Thus, the agencies cannot justify cable buys to their advertisers. And they cannot rely on any published estimates of a cable station's audience because those audiences are growing so quickly; by the time the estimates are published, they are already out of date. How can they spend a client's money when cable stations aren't even rated by Arbitron and A. C. Nielsen?

I find it amazing that agencies can so cavalierly dismiss over three thousand cable television stations simply because those stations don't play the ratings game. Already, large cable operations such as ESPN are offering advertisers rates unobtainable on network stations and also allowing advertisers more freedom to create motivating advertising, resulting in greatly increased sales figures. And when the cable stations tell the agencies they don't have rules governing commercial length and content, the agencies are flabbergasted. They are unable to adapt! Rather than exploring new advertising strategies, they simply ignore it. In the future, they will pay for that ignorance. Those agencies that learn about and become actively involved in cable now will benefit in the future. They will have established contacts and actually have a hand in shaping cable's future, growing as cable grows. Those who arrive on the cable scene too late will always be one step behind the pioneers.

The most significant system now being tested is two-way cable, a system that allows the viewer to talk back to the sender. It can be used to order merchandise, take surveys, teach classes, and there are dozens of other possibilities that can take advantage of two-way communication.

In the future, cable that involves community wiring will all but disappear. The prohibitive cost of developing this cable system extensively—spending billions of dollars to tear up streets to lay wires—makes it unfeasible.

What will be feasible is the combination of the concept of cable with the reality of satellites, producing a hybrid I call Cablite. The skies will be filled with satellites beaming down an almost infinite number of programs. These satellites will spawn a myriad of technology-related professions, and the perceptive entrepreneur will be quick to capitalize on them.

One of the most lucrative of these will be Cablite cryptography. Inevitably, Cablite transmissions will be relatively easy to bootleg unless preventative measures are taken. One of those preventatives will be to establish a cryptography system that rivals that of the military's in complexity. Technologically sophisticated decoders will be installed in subscribers' homes, and codes will often be changed on a daily basis. Such intricate systems may even involve multiple-satellite broadcast for the same program . . . each satellite responsible for a quadrant of the picture.

No one would quarrel with the statement that there are fortunes to be made in Cablite. The quarrel starts when you discuss how that money is to be made. From my perspective, money wil be made by those who master the art of the "longer" commercial. The thirty-second "entertaining" commercial will be virtually worthless within the Cablite formats. Preconceived notions of agencies and advertisers as to what constitutes an effective commercial will no longer be valid.

As opposed to present network programming, Cablite

will create a far more segmented approach. Each Cablite station will reach a much smaller and more homogeneous audience. There will be a station for every minority, every ethnic, every social, and every economic group. Cablite will take the trend in specialty magazines one step further. Not only will there be all-sports stations, but there will be all-football, -basketball, and -baseball stations. Not only will there be all-exercise stations, but there will be numerous stations with different approaches to exercising.

In addition, Cablite will usher in the age of "shopping at home" stations. These stations will air nothing but "commercials." I put "commercials" in quotes because they will bear little resemblance to most thirty-second spots now on the air. They will be much longer in length and much more straightforward in approach. And by merely pushing a button, the consumer will be able to order his groceries, his clothes, his appliances, all within a few hours. He will also pay for that product (a computer will automatically transfer money from his account or bill his credit card for the purchase). These shop-at-home stations will not merely offer consumers household items; they will run the advertising gamut, featuring everything from cars to boats to homes (this advertising might be lead-producing rather than direct-selling).

And when the FCC gives final approval to the ministation concept—which it probably will have done by the time this book is published—merchandisers will own stations. Sears, Montgomery Ward, Marshall Field will all have their own "Television Catalogs." These ministations will have only a five-mile broadcasting radius, but a major company will own hundreds of them!

All these factors will make longer commercials a fact of life. The very format of shop-at-home stations will necessitate commercials that take the time to provide all the information necessary for the potential consumer to make an immediate, educated buying decision. Fostering awareness with snappy slogans and jocular jingles won't cut it with the consumer who is a button away from making a purchase. He will have to be convinced to push that button, and detailed information about product benefits will do the convincing. And the more complex and expensive the product, the more time the advertiser will need to make the sale. For instance, a videocassette recorder manufacturer will need at least ten minutes to detail the product benefits of his recorder. Everything from the product's price to the specifics of its guarantee to a complete demonstration of all benefits of each feature will be included in the commercial. If all this is not included, the spot will fail. It will fail because the consumer will have the option of tuning in a competitor's ministation and seeing what that manufacturer has to offer in the way of videocassette recorders.

There are those who will scoff at the idea of ten-minute and longer commercials. Who is going to want to sit still and actually watch such long commercials? People who ask this question are hopelessly behind the times. They perceive television as an entertainment medium. In the Cablite future, it will have increased its power as a selling medium. Advertisers can spend ten or more minutes talking about their product without fear of viewers turning them off because the viewers will be a specialized audience; they will be turning to a channel because they want information about a product. Specialized programming will beget specialized audiences. Advertisers no longer will be sending their commercials out to a huge mass market. Their commercials will reach an audience tailor-made for the advertiser—classical records will be sold on a station that exclusively broadcasts symphonies, and electric saws will be sold on a station that conducts classes on carpentry.

In this Cablite future, shorter commercials on network stations will exist. But they will exist as "support" for the longer Cablite commercials. They will briefly inform viewers about a product or service, then direct them to the proper Cablite station for more detailed information. Increasingly, advertising will be a two-step process.

Advertising agencies that don't adapt to the new Cablite era will watch their billings plummet. Those agencies that continue to produce entertaining, award-winning commercials will be missing the boat. The agencies that grow and prosper will hire writers who are extraordinarily knowledgeable about the accounts they work on and can translate that knowledge into long, motivating commercials. Their advertising, like the old adage about a newspaper ad, will resemble a woman's skirt: short enough to be interesting, but long enough to cover the subject. Those commercials will remind some of the old pitchman commercials, in that they will be born of evolution—they will be tested and retested, written and rewritten, until the commercial is honed to perfection. Cable will allow advertisers to immediately measure sales generated by a commercial. Thus, the writer can constantly reshape the commercial until it gets maximum response.

In addition, Cablite commercials will feature "real" salespersons, not actors. As commercials shift their emphasis from entertainment to sales, so too will they shift their emphasis from spokespersons to salespersons. For instance, General Motors will find their best showroom salesman in the country, put him before the camera, and let him have the time to give his sales-producing pitch.

There is one market—more than any other—that Cablite is ideally suited to reach. In the next ten years, the average age of the United States citizen will rise dramatically according to U.S. Census forecasts. The senior citizen market will be one of the most lucrative of any era. And because senior citizens tend not to go out as much as younger people—and because many of them watch television more than younger people—their "golden years" could also be golden to the company who learns how to advertise via Cablite. With the widespread use of two-way Cablite systems, the elderly will be able to buy products without leaving their homes. In cold weather climates, especially, Cablite would be the ideal advertising vehicle to reach this burgeoning market.

And in advertising agencies, the media departments will become an increasingly important factor in the success or failure of a campaign. When Cablite stations begin multiplying the way radio stations did after World War II, media buyers must have an almost encyclopedic grasp of the most cost-effective stations. It will be virtully impossible to run fixed, thirteen week schedules on thousands of stations: to do so would mean risking millions of dollars. Instead, media buyers must arrange flexible schedules, which are renewed only if they pay out. The media supervisor must assign media buyers specialties the way a general assigns officers regiments. If this is not done, chaotic buying patterns will result. One media buyer will be responsible for Cablite ministations/direct response, another will be responsible for Cablite sports stations/retail, another will be responsible for Cablite ethnic stations, and so on. By creating media-buying specialists, agencies will ensure that media buyer and media seller work on the same team. The medium-buying specialist will be familiar with his or her territory, and establish a close working relationship with the media seller in that territory. The agencies that utilize this system will continually receive preferred rates and times on stations throughout the country.

Finally, Cablite will open the airwaves to a new generation of entrepreneurs. Two-way Cablite holds virtually limitless possibilities for those willing to experiment. In the not-so-distant future, I foresee two-way stations that develop along the same lines as stores such as Goldblatt's, Bloomingdale's, and Walgreens. Each of these stations will offer a certain type of merchandise to a certain type of subscriber. Some will feature bargains exclusively, while others will sell only the highest-quality merchandise. The discount stations will be able to offer merchandise at lower prices than any store, for they will have eliminated the middleman and such price-inflating categories as clerks, rent, pilferage, supervisory costs, expensive training, and credit losses. The flip side of the advertising coin will be the "Bloomingdale's of the Air," and they will be able to bring a daily fashion show into the subscriber's living room before the clothing is even in the stores!

For these television station "stores," subscribers lists

will be as valuable as mailing lists are to direct marketers. Rating points will mean nothing to these stations. Profits will not be determined by how many people they reach, but who those people are and when they are reached.

Perhaps the best advice I can give to those who now have or will have involvement in Cablite is this: don't base your actions on what has gone on in the past. Trying to translate standard advertising practices into Cablite is like trying to force a round peg into a square hole—it just doesn't fit. Those venturing into Cablite should use the following aphorism as a guide: Minds are like parachutes. They only function when they are open. If you don't go into Cablite with preconceived notions about how it should work—if you are able to synchronize your approach with the ultimate reality of Cablite—then you will land with your feet on very fertile ground.

16

Genesis, or How the Ad Agency Was Created in 4½ Days

In the beginning, the God-like client looked over his domain and saw his jobless son-in-law. On the first day, he said, "Let there be account supervisors." And lo, the son-in-law was an account supervisor.

And the second day, he looked at his creation and saw nothing was being done. Thus, he created the account executive from the fallen ivy leaf to help the account supervisor put his thoughts in order and run errands.

On the third day, the client thundered, "Why do I look at my blessed agency and see a vast nothingness?" And the account supervisor meekly replied, "Forgive me, Lord, but we are barren of ideas." And so, on the third day, the client created the creative department.

But the creative ones were children of darkness. They rebelled against their Lord and worshiped the pagan idol of creativity, disdaining the holy Sell. For those sins, the client banished them from his sight and created the creative director, whose sole function was to keep the creatives away from the client.

And on the fourth day, he created the media department. And verily, he said unto them, "Those of you who are Good shall become media directors." And he saw those who were Good and made them media directors, and they used their talents to shuffle papers and write memos.

And on the morning of the fifth day, the client created the research department, declaring that they would fulfill the role of scapegoat when anything went wrong. After this task, the client and agency rested.

And that is why you cannot get anyone on the phone after noon on Friday at any large Madison Avenue advertising agency.

I have written this little biblical tale not to be facetious but to make a point: many advertising agencies are structured for maximum waste and minimum effectiveness. Too often, they do everything except what they are supposed to do: sell the client's product.

The problem begins with the typical relationship between client and agency. Often, the agency literally treats the client as if he were God. They worship at the client's feet, devoting their energies and talents to keeping the client happy (and thus keeping their business) rather than honestly evaluating and implementing the best possible advertising for the client.

From this relationship, the account supervisor and executives were spawned. In most instances, they are nothing more than overpaid messenger boys shuttling between client and agency. Most have neither the analytical ability to work in the media department nor the talent to work in the creative department. Their days are spent taking clients out to lunch, explaining the fruit of the creative and media departments' labors to the client, and turning miscommunication into a science.

Ideally, an account executive should be a troubleshooter for the agency and participate in bringing in new business. In reality, however, he rarely has time or talent for either of these goals. Account executives are infrequently hired for their sales ability or even their knowledge of advertising and marketing. Instead, they are hired because they are glib, good-looking Ivy-League dressers and have MBAs (preferably from Harvard, Yale, Wharton or Stanford). In agencies, those who are salesmen often are promoted to a level where their main function is administrative rather than selling.

The complete elimination of the position of account executive would greatly facilitate the day-to-day operation of advertising agencies. By eliminating the account executive, the client and the people who "dig the ditches" of the agency would be forced to deal with each other directly, no longer relying on the middle man, the messenger, the "host." The client could talk directly to the media buyers, working with those who plan the most effective media-buying strategy; he could talk directly to the writers who create his ads, ensuring that all of them are operating on the same wavelength.

Additionally, the elimination of the account executive would ameliorate much internal tension within agencies, tension that is counterproductive to good advertising. Traditionally, account executives and creatives have an adversary relationship. They fight each other for control of the account, each wanting to claim responsibility of a campaign when it succeeds and disclaim responsibility when it fails. As a result, they spend much of their time bickering with one another rather than working for the client.

The responsibilities of the account executive (though most never fulfill those responsibilities) can easily be disseminated to others within an agency. Those responsible for selling a campaign to a client or for getting new business should be drawn from teams of highly trained, top-level executives within the agency, men and women with the experience and ability to sell. They should have first gained their experience on the client side so they have a dual perspective to bring to their accounts. They should also have spent time in the field so they understand the nuts-and-bolts aspects of marketing a product.

In structuring an agency, it is essential that media buyers be chosen for their ability to sell, because it is their job to sell the media on giving them the best exposure for the client expenditure. Many large agencies make the mistake of promoting superior media buyers into supervisory capacities (or, heaven forbid, even up the ladder to account executive), thereby not only wasting their abilities, but also leaving their media-buying departments barren of talent. To help good media buyers remain media buyers, agencies should provide them with the increased responsibility, security, and salaries they are entitled to. If this is done, not only can an agency establish solid working relationships with the media representatives, but they can become involved in their prime objective—moving merchandise for the client.

Creative departments at many large agencies have always reminded me of an untended garden—too many weeds among the flowers. These agencies often have talented people working in their creative departments, but that talent never blossoms because it is choked off by a chain of command that dictates concept. Too often, the writers and artists become robots of the bureaucratic hierarchy. Once again, direct contact between artist, writer, and the client could facilitate communication and result in advertising that reflects the client's main objective: to sell product.

Creative departments should be streamlined for maximum effectiveness. To create effective broadcast advertising, all writers should be producers and all producers should be writers. If the writer produces his own creation, then the end result will be exactly what the writer intended, free from the aesthetic standards a producer imposed (which often waters down the selling message). The writer/producer should deal directly with the client, presenting his concepts. After all, who can better explain an ad than the person who wrote it?

In addition, writer/producers should not be isolated from the selling/marketing process. Too often, agencies isolate their creative people, letting them dwell in the realm of ideas instead of the world of profit and loss. They should be encouraged to learn everything there is to know about the product they write about—where it is distributed, how it's manufactured, who their audience is. Only then will they be able to sell product rather than win awards.

And finally, there are research departments. As I have stated in previous chapters, the only research that I have ever given any great credibility to is post-analytical research—research that tells you what has happened, not what might happen. This "might happen," "theoretical," research too often is the foundation of research departments.

Theoretical research is a defense mechanism, providing the client with the justification for his decisions and the agency for its marketing strategy. To eliminate this dependence on research would save the client a great deal of time and money. In fact, common sense often can be profitably substituted for research. One of the best examples of common sense triumphing over research occurred when we were hired by an auto club to test TV's ability to obtain new members. Our first exposure to the club was a research session at which the researchers explained that the primary reason for joining a motor club was "security."

Being new to the account—and not wanting to show my ignorance by interrupting with questions—I waited until the presentation was over to ask the client what was meant by "security." I couldn't understand it. After all, if one did belong to the motor club, one could still get a flat tire on a busy highway at night . . . one still had to make a phone call . . . one could still be robbed.

My question surprised the client. No one knew what the researchers meant by the word "security."

I smiled and said, "You can spend a billion dollars in research, but there's only one reason anybody joins a motor club. He expects to get more from it than the cost of membership. He's out to beat you. He knows that if he has to call the wrecker once, it would normally cost him more than his membership fee. He joins a 'prevention' club only to beat the game." That's just common sense.

While most agencies could benefit from the subtraction of a research department, they could also benefit from the addition of a Product Review Board. The PRB should be composed of representatives of the creative, media, and accounting departments as well as the top executives within the agency. Its function would be to evaluate new and existing clients' products and concepts. The PRB would determine the product's chances for success. They would evaluate every aspect of it—from packaging and pricing to positioning and mode of distribution. They would play devil's advocate, running a product through a gauntlet of questions. By the time they had finished their analysis, no stone would be unturned. Every potential problem could be solved before the product was even mass-produced. With the benefit of a PRB's foresight, costly advertising and marketing mistakes could be greatly reduced.

The structure of many advertising agencies has not changed with the times. With few exceptions, they are organized the same way they were forty years ago.

A new agency organizational chart could be easily designed and implemented, using what I call the "team" approach.

A client should be assigned a creative team, a media team, and a marketing team. The members of each team would be responsible for planning and executing work for the client and would meet directly with the client. If the client and team cannot work out a problem (this would be rare), an agency troubleshooter would be called in to solve it. This team approach would facilitate communications between client and agency, eliminating scores of middlemen and administrators (account execs, account supervisors, creative directors, media supervisors).

Many agencies might like to think they use this team approach presently, but I think they are mistaken. Their "teams" are too large, consisting of a hierarchy of supervisors and more supervisors. In these agencies, the people who do the actual buying of time and writing of ads aren't ever on these "teams." And often, the media "team" has no idea what the creative "team" is doing.

In the ideal team structure, the separate teams would coordinate their work. The marketing strategy for a client would fit the creative strategy like a glove. Because these teams would have the responsibility for making important decisions, they would have a greater incentive to ensure that those decisions were the right ones. Thus, the team approach would result in greater agency efficiency and diligence.

And as many of you know, those are two qualities clients complain are missing from the agencies they employ.

17

In Defense
of Direct Marketing*

Woman (screaming):
**"You crooks cashed my check and I never
got my records. Either you send them today
or I'm reporting you to the post office,
Better Business Bureau, Consumer Fraud
Department . . . I'll sue your company for every
cent you've got!"**

What direct marketer hasn't watched this scene played out
time and again? The irate phone call from a dissatisfied customer is as common to the business as toll-free numbers.
Occasionally, the phone call is justified. Many times, however, the call comes from a consumer intent on getting
something for nothing. And most often, he gets it.

One reason for this is the general perception of the
direct-marketing industry. It is watched more closely than
the most dangerous criminal. Numerous federal and local
agencies track the direct marketer's every step, ready to
pounce at the slightest hint of any wrongdoing. So, when
that caller complains, the DM is as nervous as a long-tailed
cat in a roomful of rocking chairs.

Perhaps the government's overzealous attitude is justified. The public should be protected from a handful of un-

---

scrupulous direct marketers. But who protects marketers from the unscrupulous public? Certainly not the government. By their seeming indifference to the problems direct marketers face, they give tacit approval to every budding con artist scheming to bilk a company out of a product or money.

Direct marketers lose an estimated $300 million each year because of these con artists. And for each con artist, there is a different con. Here are a few examples: (1) People who claim they sent in their money for a product and didn't receive it; (2) people who claim they never received a product when in fact they did; (3) those who send in phony orders as a joke, and when the product is delivered, do not accept it; (4) those who say they sent their product in for a refund and never received it; (5) the product is stolen by either a postal official or someone who sees it outside a door; (6) people who deliberately misuse a product and send it back, taking advantage of the money-back guarantee.

What is so insidious about these cons is that they're virtually foolproof. Direct marketers routinely send both money and product back to those who complain. They do so because the ominous threat of a lawsuit or FTC interference is behind every call; because mistakes are made— letters lost, checks misplaced—the complaint might be legitimate; because it's the easiest thing to do. A loss of $4.95 won't break any company, especially one that does a high-volume business.

But of course, those losses add up. And the consumer, as well as the direct marketer, ends up a loser. Prices of items must be upped as much as 25 percent to compensate for these losses.

Can anything be done? Well, the first and easiest thing to do is for direct marketers to conduct a public relations campaign, explaining to consumers the negative aspect of cheating a direct marketer. Too often, people view this cheating as harmless as stealing towels from a motel: Who does it hurt? After all, they've got plenty. I call these people mail-order kleptomaniacs. Often, they order something by mail, knowing full well they will receive the item, and ignore the bill that follows. These people have to be made aware that they are ultimately hurting themselves.

On another level, the government has to be made aware of the problems direct marketers face. An effective lobbying effort would be a good start to solve government apathy. This lobbying effort should act as a catalyst for the creation of an independent watchdog group that would ferret out those who attempt to defraud direct marketers. This would act as a central clearinghouse, supplying direct marketers with the names of repeat offenders. Such a list would cut fraud almost in half.

Finally, this whole situation is exacerbated by something neither consumers not direct marketers have any control over. From reading a variety of studies, I would estimate that 20 percent of products ordered by people in inner-city areas is never delivered. The reason: both United Parcel and post office employees often refuse to venture into "bad" neighborhoods and attempt to collect C.O.D. They are not entirely to blame when you consider that police often are reluctant to enter public housing projects for any reason. The problem, however, is that these postal employees cover themselves by reporting that the customer wasn't at home. Hence the legitimate complaints from inner-city dwellers. And so a hue and cry is raised and the direct marketer is its object. Yet he is powerless to stop this mail-order redlining.

Obviously, there is no easy answer to the problem. But the wrong answer is to say nothing can be done. That will only encourage those who cheat direct marketers to continue to do so. Since some of you reading this are experts in the art of selling, perhaps you could use your talents to sell both the public and government on the need for action. I'm sure you'll get an overwhelming response.

18

Conclusion

This book has covered a great deal of territory, ranging from the pitchman past to the Cablite future. Chapters have been devoted to everything from how to be a successful entrepreneur to how to create the ultimate selling commercial. Certain topics I have discussed related to direct marketing, while others related to retailing.

Despite the diversity of style and substance within this book, there is an underlying theme that pertains to everything I've written and to everyone reading this. Whether you are an advertising agency executive or a Fortune 500 company president or an industrial manufacturer or a chain-store operator or an inventor or a consumer, there is one message I wish to convey above all else: Tradition is one of the greatest deterrents to progress.

In the world of advertising and marketing, reliance on traditional methods is ultimately fatal—fatal to a businessman's career, a product, even an entire company. Those who rely on tradition will continually avoid innovation, modernization, and growth. They will not be able to change with the changing times.

Therefore, I am dismayed when I see agencies and advertisers making the same mistakes day in and day out simply because they did it that way yesterday; or because they tried that "untraditional" approach in 1962 and it didn't work so they refuse to try again (whenever someone says that to me in a meeting, I always respond, "I don't suppose you have any children"). Too many advertisers and agencies create unmotivating advertising because they are bound to the tradition of awards, theoretical research, prime-time buys, and bureaucratic hierarchies. And they are horrified by such untraditional approaches as the theory of sales resistance, the isolation factor, and Key Outlet Marketing.

The problem in many agencies and companies is that the entrepreneur is no longer the policy maker. I am talking about the entrepreneur who started the company, who had that spark of intuition that often took precedence over logic. In many cases, he has been replaced by the MBA, whose business decisions are governed only by tradition and logic—logic that prevents him from understanding why ratings or cost per thousand, for example, should not be the only criterion in buying television time.

At this point, I should clarify the difference between tradition and experience. Tradition means doing something today because that is the way it has always been done. Experience is the realization that it doesn't work that way anymore. Unfortunately, the new generation of management is often short on experience and long on tradition. They use tradition as a crutch, leaning too heavily upon it for support. It's safe to justify one's actions by saying, "Well, that's the way it's always been done." Though this approach might provide someone with an excuse when things don't work, it doesn't provide the motivation to take risks that is necessary for progress.

In the near future, the business world will undergo numerous, significant changes. And the more things change, the more unfeasible traditional methods become. For instance, one of the most significant changes will be the installation of sophisticated computer systems in virtually every individual retail store operation in the country. These computers will be able to feed a central computer with day-to-day movement reports for the advertisers.

For the first time, advertisers will have a foolproof method of measuring how their advertising affects sales. Once a campaign breaks, they can look at daily computer printouts and determine whether that campaign is affecting sales positively or negatively. Agencies will no longer be allowed the luxury of such traditional practices as running long, unproductive advertising schedules and relying on awards, high recall scores, or brand awareness as the criteria for the measurement of success. When the printout gives a market-by-market, store-by-store, hour-by-hour breakdown of a product's sales, none of the traditional barometers of advertising's effectiveness will mean anything.

When this widespread system of computers is a reality, agencies and advertisers will be forced to restructure their advertising, marketing, and merchandising strategies. Those strategies will be forced to become more flexible and innovative, adaptable to a sudden change in sales results. Agencies will have to be able to write and produce a new commercial at the drop of a hat . . . or the drop of sales. Advertisers will have to have a first-person direct line with the agency media buyers who place their advertising—how else can they react swiftly and effectively to adapt their media-buying strategies to the fluctuating sales in each market?

With all due modesty, I would like to think that I have laid the groundwork for some of the untraditional approaches that will be used in the future. The "alternative" media buying, marketing, and creative techniques I have discussed in this book are designed solely to maximize sales. In the computerized, cablized future, that will be an advertiser's only consideration.

In fact, I can see a day in the future when these untraditional approaches become—dare I use the word—"traditional." When that happens, I hope a new generation of entrepreneurs will challenge the status quo. I hope that there will always be some brazen young entrepreneur who has the courage to make such an untraditional statement as "Satisfaction Guaranteed or Your Money Back."

Appendix A:
A Word about the Knock-off Syndrome

What happened to the electric toothbrush, the Shower Massage, the electric knife, the Crock-Pot? Were they merely fads, products that enjoyed a brief moment in the spotlight and then vanished from view because they exhausted their market?

The aforementioned products—as well as many others—were victims of what we call the knock-off syndrome. It is as deadly to an innovative product as d-Con was and is to rats. In a matter of months, a successful product can have its market cut out from under it, and in some cases, the entire product category can be wiped out.

It begins when a new product is introduced to the marketplace. Its extensive advertising campaign—which educates the public and heralds its uniqueness and consumer benefits—is responsible for the product's success. Of course, merchandising and advertising a new product requires markup so all this can be done. As soon as sales start to soar, however, numerous manufacturers jump on the bandwagon and rush to bring out their parade of knock-offs. In some instances, the products are legitimate—well made and fairly priced. But often these knock-offs are of lower quality and are lower priced than the original product and only claim to do what the original product actually does. When these knock-offs start appearing, they do a brisk business; many buyers shun the high-priced originator for the lower-priced copy. Sales of the original product begin to drop off. The originator's advertising—which was instrumental in fostering awareness of his unique new product—is cut back. Soon, all advertising for the category stops. In a short time, both the original and the knock-off products stop selling!

The knock-offs stop manufacturing and withdraw from the market, but the game is over. The originator is afraid to go back to his intensive advertising campaign because the knock-offs are standing in the wings waiting for the advertising to begin again so they can dump their inventory. In many cases, within a few months both the originals and knock-offs disappear from the shelves.

There are many variations on the knock-off theme. Consider what happened when General Electric introduced the original electric knife at $24.95. For two years, their advertising worked overtime to educate the public to the need for and uses of their new product. Gradually, the idea took hold in the consumers' minds, and GE found itself with a highly successful product. In less than a year, however, no less than sixty-five companies flooded the market with electric knives ranging in price from $4.95 to $19.95.

Greedy chains and department stores put all products side by side in their newly established "electric knife department." Because GE couldn't afford the advertising to move these competitive products, they cut back their advertising. The entire category dropped 86 percent in sales in less than one year and the chains, experiencing only one fleeting moment of success, had killed the goose that laid the golden egg.

The electric toothbrush suffered a similar fate. Shortly after its introduction, more than five hundred knock-offs flooded the market. And again, within a year, a multimillion-dollar product category dropped by 75 percent.

Other victims of the knock-off syndrome include the tabletop rotisserie, the electric frying pan, the Crock-Pot, the deep fryer, Shower Massage, the auto-sun visor, food chopper, and even the yo-yo!

What is so shameful about the knock-off situation is that it can be prevented. Retailers merely have to understand that knock-offs are detrimental to their profits in the long run, and refuse to stock knock-offs.

The unusual aspect of the knock-off syndrome is that after all the smoke clears away, few manufacturers of knock-offs have made any profit, and the only product left on the shelf is the high-priced originator and one or two knock-offs that competed for quality, not for price. In the case of the electric toothbrush, only GE, Broxodent, Sunbeam, and Teledyne have products available in any quantity because most of the knock-offs were not priced with adequate margin for the advertising necessary to sustain the market.

When A. Eicoff & Company took on a new product called Handi-Screen, we had great hopes for it. It was a screen that covered pans and prevented grease from spurting out of the pan onto the stovetop or onto the person who was doing the cooking. There was nothing similar to it in the marketplace, it served a valuable purpose, and it could be sold for only $3 with an adequate, built-in budget for advertising.

In the first year, 4 million Handi-Screens were sold, which translates roughly into $12 million in retail sales. Then, a series of competitors introduced similar products at a similar price. When they were unable to obtain much retail distribution, they desperately tried to recover this investment in inventory by offering the knock-offs for $1, and retailers were quick to grab the close-out. The result: soon the market was flooded with low-priced close-outs, which resulted in the demise of the category. Retailers lost what could have been an annual sales category of at least $12 million.

Smart buyers, however, are beginning to understand the inherent danger of knock-offs.

When we introduced the Roll-O-Matic mop, the first

no-stoop, no-bend, self-wringing mop, it retailed for $9.95. Though it was priced higher than most kitchen mops, its price was justified by its unique features and benefits. Still, as sales increased, we knew the Roll-O-Matic mop would be prey to the knock-off artist.

Our worst fears soon came to pass. Within a short period of time, a number of competitors introduced similar mops. Because these competitors did not have adequate advertising budgets (relying on Roll-O-Matic advertising to establish product awareness and draw customers to the stores), they were able to sell the mop for less than the Roll-O-Matic.

Smart retailers had learned their lessons, however, and refused to stock the knock-offs. Many were farsighted enough to realize that the "quick-kills" they might make on the knock-offs would ultimately kill off the entire category. The few major chains that stocked the knock-offs realized that they only reduced their profits, and they quickly discontinued buying them.

Because of the foresight of wise merchandisers, the Roll-O-Matic mop continues to prosper, and it is able to maintain both its distribution and price level.

I am not caviling against knock-offs because they represent competition. I am a strong advocate of competition—the kind of competition that benefits the manufacturer, the product, and the consumer. In its most ideal form, competition forces manufacturers and ad agencies to create an informative, motivating commercial; and it forces the public to evaluate a product and act upon that evaluation.

When one of my clients decides to knock-off a product, I always advise him to price it higher than the original, rather than lower. This gives him the markup to make a top-quality product and necessary funds to properly advertise and merchandise it. And, I always emphasize that when the smoke clears away, only the higher-priced products are left in the market.

Appendix B:
Send in Your Name and Address and $1.98

In the late forties my first big job was for Marfree Advertising, a New York firm that represented a number of small radio stations. It was virtually impossible to convince any national broadcast advertisers to buy time on these stations because the stations had neither the power nor the ratings to satisfy those advertisers. The only interest I could generate was among direct marketers—the people who ran mail-order ads in pulp magazines.

The problem was that most print-oriented direct marketers didn't have experience in broadcast. As a result, I found myself transformed into a combination copywriter/media buyer for those accounts that I convinced to try broadcast. I soon learned that the stations I represented were too small to pull any volume of mail with direct-response offers, so I began searching for stations that had the power, coverage, programming, and know-how to pull orders.

My mentor was Charles Topmiller of WCKY in Cincinnati; he showed me the media-buying and copywriting ropes. He also introduced me to the smartest, shrewdest direct-marketing radio executives in the country, including: Fred Hamm, WJJD, Chicago; Blackie Blackman, WLAC, Nashville; Ben Ludy, WIBW, Topeka; Paul Miller, WWVA, Wheeling; and John Hopkins, the American representative for most of the leading Mexican border stations.

I parlayed these contacts and my newfound knowledge of direct-response advertising into my first bona-fide success: a direct-response offer of sixteen used jukebox phonograph records (an offer I got through Galgano Records of Chicago).

I found I had a natural talent for writing radio commercials. My technique was simple. Before I wrote the first word, I asked myself: "What would it take to sell me this product?" What claim would motivate me to write a letter and enclose a check? Then I wrote the copy to sell myself!

The technique worked. At one point I had six of the leading direct-response offers on radio: (1) The Quilt Lady, 3 pounds of fabric remnants to make crazy quilts; (2) Galgano Records; (3) d-Con; (4) Pinto, a plastic pony with a noisemaker; (5) an offer for harmonica lessons; and (6) Dean Ross Piano Lessons. At one time I reached billings of $125,000 a week in P.I.s and had only one employee. My success was the catalyst for a country and western song written about me called: "Send in Your Name and Address and $1.98."

My success was not unique. This was the boom time for radio direct-response offers, and a number of agencies used direct marketing in radio to rake in profits. The largest was O'Neill, Larson & McMahon, and two of the partners were a genius copywriter named Ed McMahon and a brilliant media expert, Walter Zivy. Their products included everything from ballpoint pens (Penman) to Serutan (Nature spelled backward). There was also Schafer, Brennan, Margulis of Saint Louis (whose son is David Margulis, presently a VP at Ogilvy & Mather). They were responsible for the success of Black's Baby Chicks (100 chicks for $2.98), Heilbros watches, and Aglow (a picture of the Last Supper that glowed in the dark). Other leading direct-response heavyweights included Harry Schneiderman (Mason Shoes), Harold Schwartz of the ad agency that bore his name, and Maury Bronner of Olian & Bronner, whose major offer was 100 razor blades for $1.

During this era Maury Bronner and Harold Kay combined their talents to establish "The Mail Order Radio Network," which consisted of the largest radio stations in the country. There was no single announcer or telephone line that united the network, but they were combined through a central clearinghouse that would test and then accept or reject direct-response items from various agencies. The network began at 11:00 P.M. and signed off at 6:00 A.M. It wasn't unusual for stations like WOR, New York; WGN, Chicago; and KNOX, Saint Louis, to pull 10,000 orders per week for a single product. I had a record offer that contained "Tennessee Waltz," "Daddy's Little Girl," and "Beyond the Sunset." The Monday that it aired 23,000 orders were waiting at WCKY in Cincinnati. The mail-order network pulled another 32,000.

The formats of the top direct-response stations were remarkably similar. They had either a country and western or a middle-of-the-road pop format. They all used a thirty-second opening, a two-minute middle commercial, and a sixty-second close in a ten-minute segment. They were actually devoting twenty-one minutes per hour to commercials! And all their announcers had one indispensable trait in common. Each one of them—Randy Blake of WJJD, Chicago; Don Davis and Nelson King on WCKY, Cincinnati;· Irv Victor on KNOX, Saint Louis and WGN, Chicago—could deliver more than 200 words per minute and make it sound as if they were talking at a snail's pace. The result: The commercials could be loaded with benefit-oriented motivating information.

This golden era of radio was not to last, however. When television made its debut, radio stations panicked. They feared they were overcommercialized and therefore would lose listeners to the relatively commercial-free television stations. Their paranoia caused them to declare certain hours and even certain weeks commercial-free.

Radio stations then made another decision that added

to their problems. They decided to limit commercial length to sixty seconds.

This double-barreled blast knocked direct-response advertisers off the radio. Not only was the successful direct-response format suddenly gone, but there was not even enough time to repeat and repeat the mailing address so that it would be firmly embedded in the listeners' minds.

Television, of course, was waiting in the wings, and it eventually picked up more than $250,000,000 annually in direct-response advertising!

As the years passed, a new generation of radio management came to power. The neophyte station managers did not understand (or had never been exposed to) direct marketing. They didn't understand that a direct marketer buys only one week of advertising and that he won't renew a schedule that doesn't deliver orders at a profitable level. They didn't understand the very concept of P.I.s (Per Inquiry), which provided stations with a ''cash library'' of commercials that could be scheduled in any unsold time to provide additional income they wouldn't have had under normal conditions.

During the last decade television management has made it a point to understand and work with direct marketers, and it has greatly profited from them. It's time for their radio counterparts to wise up and clean up their acts! Direct marketers and their agencies are actively searching for alternative media outlets. Television is approaching the saturation point—only a finite number of two-minute slots are available—and there are gallons of spillover advertising dollars. Radio has the capability to absorb that spillover.

In a recession, direct marketers prosper. Because many people don't have the discretionary income to go out, they tend to stay home and listen to the radio or watch television, thereby increasing the audience for direct-response offers.

More than any other medium, radio is in the position to take advantage of this growing audience. It offers the direct marketer an unbeatable combination: the immediacy of broadcast and the selective audience of print. The ingredients that make narrow-cast cable attractive to direct marketers are also present in radio.

What distinguishes radio, however, is its total reliance on sound to communicate a message. Certain direct-response products lend themselves to audio rather than video presentations; their benefits cannot be demonstrated as well to the eye as to the mind. By painting word pictures about these products (or services), the advertiser allows the listener to fantasize about them. Radio's power—both as a selling and as an entertainment medium—is generated by the listener's imagination.

Each day brings scores of new direct-response products into the marketplace, many of which are ideally suited for radio. To take advantage of these new products, radio stations must actively solicit this business. To do so, they must immediately dispense with the one-minute ceiling for direct-response commercials. Consider that television has a two-minute limit but can use timesaving pictures, whereas radio has to rely on time-consuming words.

Perhaps radio should borrow a page from its own history. In the halcyon days of direct-response radio, a direct-response offer was segmented within a sponsored ten- or fifteen-minute format. It began with a thirty-second opening—the holder—that set forth the offer: "In just a few minutes, I'm going to tell you about a revolutionary new invention that's half the size of a fountain pen that you can put in your pocket. It will keep flies, gnats, and mosquitos more than ten feet from you no matter how bad the infestation. But first, let's listen to. . . ." Normal programming then resumed. Five minutes later, a two-minute commercial aired, explaining the benefits of the product and repeating the phone number and address (to place an order) at least four times. Again, regular programming resumed. Finally, a one-minute commercial summarized the offer and repeated the address and phone number two more times.

This "segmented" approach to radio direct response could be successfully implemented today. It could take the form of sponsorship of newscasts, take shows, or any number of different programming modes. The alternating rhythm of commercials and regular programming are complementary: People interested in the offer have an added incentive to listen to the program, and people interested in the program get two or three chances to respond to the offer. And finally, this format would allow the direct marketer to reach a highly targeted audience—the advertising would be woven seamlessly into the show, reaching people predisposed to buy the product.

When should radio direct-response offers run? They should follow the same guidelines set forth in this book for television: early morning, late evening, and weekends. Under no circumstances should a direct-response radio commercial air during the expensive 6:30 A.M. to 9:00 A.M. or 4:30 P.M. to 7:00 P.M. drive-time periods. It is obviously difficult for a person to write down an address or to make a phone call while driving to or from work.

All this is not to say that direct marketers should forsake print and television advertising. Rather, radio can be used in conjunction with other media. In this second golden era of direct-response advertising, there are enough media dollars for everybody. Direct marketers searching for imaginative, effective alternatives recognize radio's potential as a direct-response vehicle. The only question is: When will radio stations recognize their own potential?

Glossary

ADI: Area of Dominant Influence.

ANDY: An annual award given to the most entertaining TV commercials, not the ones that generate the most sales.

AVENUE OF HARLOTS: The street on which the advertising wheeler-dealers dwell.

BIORHYTHMS: The actual physical and psychological changes a person undergoes over a period of time.

BRAND AWARENESS: As determined by Burke Scores, the percentage of those able to remember the name of a product and at least one selling point after viewing that product's commercial.

CABLE: A wire connected to a television set that changes the quality or quantity of programs received.

CABLITE: The combination of the concept of cable with the reality of satellites.

CASH LIBRARY: A series of commercials that stations can run when they have an opening; time that otherwise would have been wasted becomes net profit.

CLIO: An award similar to ANDY.

CLOSE-OUT MAN: The person who buys up bankrupt, discontinued, or apparently unsalable merchandise at a small fraction of the manufacturing cost.

CPM (COST PER THOUSAND): The dollar cost of media primarily used in determining audience.

CUME: Cumulative or unduplicated coverage—the total number of different people you reach.

DAYTIME DIRECTIONAL: A radio station granted a license to operate only during daylight hours, with multiple antennas that block its signal from specified areas.

DEMOGRAPHICS: Measurements of socioeconomic classifications.

DIRECT MARKETING: The sale of product or service by the advertisers directly to consumer without use of a retail outlet (what the seller does).

DIRECT RESPONSE: The direct ordering of product or service by mail or phone without use of a retail outlet (what the buyer does).

FIRM: A contract you must honor from start to finish, that doesn't contain a cancellation clause.

FLASH: Everything necessary for a pitchman to demonstrate a product.

FOCUS GROUP: A group of people who are given a "concept" ad and asked to comment upon it. This is used by agencies to determine the strength of their creative departments.

HAWTHORNE EFFECT (from the Hawthorne Works of the Western Electric Co., Cicero, Illinois, where its existence was established by experiment): The stimulation to increase output or accomplishment (as in an industrial or educational methods study) that results from the mere fact of being under concerned observation; also: such an increase in output or accomplishment.

HOLDER: A promise or an action on the part of the pitchman to keep an audience from walking away (or "tuning out" the commercial).

IMPULSE PURCHASE: Purchase of a product catalyzed by mere sighting of product in store, not motivated by advertising.

IN-OUT PROMOTION: The promotion of a specific item for a specific length of time. The unsold merchandise is returned to the advertiser no matter how successful the promotion might have been.

INVESTMENT SPENDING: Advertising dollars spent on media on assumption that they will produce profits at some future date.

ISOLATION FACTOR: The positive sales effect of running a commercial by itself (as opposed to running a commercial in a cluster).

JOINT: Any product or service sold by a pitchman.

KEY OUTLET MARKETING: The distribution of a product into a

selected chain or chains in an individual market. Each market is handled as a profit center and ad schedules are renewed on a market-by-market basis after the market has shown a profit for the advertised product.

KNOCK-OFF: A copy of a successful and highly promoted item by another manufacturer who doesn't have to amortize the high cost of new product introduction.

LARRY: A product that doesn't perform well.

MAGIC NUMBER: The maximum advertising allowable per unit sold to return an acceptable profit to the advertiser.

MAIL ORDER: A product or service offered to the consumer through the mail.

MOOCH: A buyer of what the pitchman is selling.

NEGATIVE RECALL: The extent to which a commercial motivates the consumer not to buy the product advertised.

PARALLEL STRUCTURE TECHNIQUE (PST): A creative strategy whereby a commercial shows two parallel situations—one without the product and one with it.

P.I. (PER INQUIRY): Contract for advertising that calls for payment to the medium to be determined only by the actual sales that medium produces.

POINT-OF-SALE DISPLAY: The display the retail store gives to a specific product.

POSITIONING: A creative strategy used to determine how the consumer perceives a product; a product may be "positioned" as inexpensive, glamorous, trendy, etc.

POSITIVE RECALL: The extent to which a commercial motivates the consumer to buy the product advertised.

PRIME ACCESS: The hour immediately preceding or following the prime-time period.

PRODUCT MARKETING INDEX (PMI): A scientific guide that enables advertisers to determine how much to spend in any given market to move X number of units of product.

RATINGS: The number of TV or radio homes tuned to a specific station at a specific time. Each rating is 1 percent of the total number of TV or radio homes in that market.

REACH: The unduplicated audience in a given TV coverage area.

REEL: A "portfolio" of a writer or art director's best commercials used to get a job at an advertising agency.

RETURN PRIVILEGE: The right of a retail outlet to return merchandise that they don't sell (guaranteed sale).

ROP: Runs of paper, which means paper has choice of placing ad in any section they want as opposed to advertiser saying where he wants it placed.

SLICE-OF-LIFE COMMERCIAL: Commercial that attempts to simulate a real-life situation through the use of short, dramatic vignettes.

SPOT: A commercial.

SUPPORT ADVERTISING: The use of a secondary medium whose sole purpose is to call attention to an ad appearing in the primary medium.

THEORY OF SALES RESISTANCE: There are times of the day and days of the week when an advertiser can more easily sell his product, and there are times of the day and days of the week when an advertiser finds it difficult to sell his product.

TIP: The audience gathered by a pitchman.

TURN: The point in any commercial or pitch where the product demonstration ends and asking for the order begins.

TWO-WAY CABLE: Cable that allows the viewer to respond directly to the sender by merely pushing a button.

UNIQUE SELLING PROPOSITION (USP): Any benefit that differentiates a product from its competitors, ranging from packaging to performance to price.

UNIVERSAL DISTRIBUTION: Distribution of a product in every possible outlet that should sell the product and occasionally in outlets that shouldn't be selling it.

Index